The Twists of a Brain

Gene Smith

The Twists of a Brain

By
Betty J. Smith

www.STL-Books.com

Cover art work by Lauren Smith

bluebird
PUBLISHING
St. Louis MO, 63108

Contents

Foreword		7
Preface		10
Chapter 1	Our Life Before	17
Chapter 2	Beginnings	26
Chapter 3	Hearing Aids	34
Chapter 4	Early Signs	36
Chapter 5	Houston	39
Chapter 6	Stockholder's Meeting	42
Chapter 7	Frustration	45
Chapter 8	Washington University	53
Chapter 9	More Changes	56
Chapter 10	Friends	62
Chapter 11	Routines	66
Chapter 12	Duffy's	68
Chapter 13	Wednesday Club	71
Chapter 14	Gracie	75
Chapter 15	Skaneateles	78
Chapter 16	Caregivers	82
Chapter 17	Practice Trips	86
Chapter 18	Nursing Homes	92
Chapter 19	Nightmare	97
Chapter 20	End Days	108
Epilogue		117
Case History		121
Acknowledgements		125
About The Author		128

Our children, Tom, Dave & Carol,
and all our family and friends
who traveled this road with us.

Foreword

Alzheimer's disease (AD) is a relentlessly progressive disorder that causes brain cells to degenerate and die. When a critical number of cells in a particular brain region are affected, brain functioning increasingly is impaired. The brain regions that are most vulnerable to the Alzheimer process subserve functions that impart our human qualities: self-knowledge, memory, reasoning, personality, and language.

The familiar symptoms of AD thus include forgetfulness ("short-term memory loss"), confusion, and personality changes. The onset of symptoms is insidious so that it is difficult to know precisely when the illness begins, but inexorably there is worsening such that the affected individual gradually becomes unable to perform his or her usual activities.

In the later stages of AD, the ability to conduct even basic activities such as toileting and feeding are lost. It should be a national imperative to support and fund research in AD to discover the reasons why brain cells deteriorate so that truly effective treatments can be developed. Otherwise, the ever-growing number of older adults who are at greatest risk for the disorder will ensure a pandemic of AD that will overwhelm our health care system.

For all that has been learned about this disease, it remains true that "when you have seen one case of Alzheimer's, you've seen one case of Alzheimer's." Each affected individual presents with their own special constellation of symptoms and signs, and how the illness is experienced by their family and friends also is unique. Nonetheless, in virtually all situations AD affects not just the patient but the entire family. In more than 25 years of seeing patients with AD, I never cease to be impressed by the loving and supportive care that is provided by spouses, children, and other family members. However, the burden of being the primary caregiver almost always falls to the person closest to the individual.

In *The Twists of a Brain*, Betty J. Smith provides a moving and engrossing memoir that simply and effectively relates the devastation that AD brought to her life and her affected husband, Gene. Her experiences are very instructive for all who must cope with this terrible disorder. The book also serves to describe a variant form of AD, in which language difficulties rather than memory loss were the first and most prominent symptoms of the illness. At its heart, however, *The Twists of a Brain* is a love story. Readers will easily appreciate how much Betty and Gene Smith loved one another, and how that love was manifested so clearly as together they shared the burden of Alzheimer's disease. In doing so, they have inspired us all.

John C. Morris, M.D.
Harvey A. and Dorismae Hacker Friedman
Distinguished Professor of Neurology
Professor of Pathology and Immunology
Professor of Physical Therapy
Professor of Occupational Therapy
Director, ADRC
Director, Center for Aging
Director, Memory and Aging Project

Preface

It was our usual stop before he took me home from class. We sat in his car, a fifties Studebaker, at the Parkmoor restaurant — it had curb service then. Screaming brakes and the pitiful cry of a dog interrupted our conversation. A young beagle (I had a beagle at home named Muffet) had been hit by a car in the middle of traffic on busy Clayton Road. Gene immediately got out of his car, stopped the traffic, and rescued the dog by carrying it to a grassy section. He was so caring and, as my heart went out to the dog, I fell in love with Gene. I later found out that he liked cats, too. What a guy!

Gene and I met at Washington University at the beginning of my freshman year and his junior. He was sitting at a table, working at registration, and a friend introduced us. He stood up and my first impression was that he was very tall. Actually he was only 6" but skinny, and I'm 5'2"; so he was very tall to me.

About a week later, this same friend said that Gene was going to ask me out and I was delighted. I waited for his call and he asked me out for the next Saturday night. Oh dear, I already had a date. He said, "How about Friday night?" Oh dear, I already had a date! I didn't have a date for the football game, and I didn't know how to tell him that. But I sure wanted him to take me to the football game. Now I think God had plans for this romance because a few days later, the guy I had a date with Saturday night called and said he had to cancel, but a fraternity brother would like to take me out. I asked, "Who was it?" Oh my, it was Gene Smith! The phone rang immediately after I hung up, and it was Gene.

It wasn't love at first sight but it grew and grew. Then at Parkmoor that afternoon as Gene cared for that puppy, love truly blossomed. He was a gentle, fun loving, caring person.

It was summertime 1954 and we were walking along a street full of shops, lingering in front of the windows sparkling with rings. We had been pinned — he was a Phi Delta Theta and I was a Delta Gamma — since October and he was due to leave for the army in July.

Oh, joy! We decided to pick out a ring and he put money down on it. We agreed we would announce our engagement when he came home on leave.

Letters arrived to me almost every day that fall from Fort Belvoir, where Gene was a 2nd lieutenant in the Corps of Engineers. Our engagement party before Christmas at my parents' home was quite bittersweet. Gene was going to Nurenberg Germany, and I wouldn't see him again until July 1956.

Betty and Gene along Grand Avenue in St. Louis, 1954.

We married in 1956 and had a wonderful life together, three super kids, who all married supportive spouses and we now have eight delightful grandchildren. As I write this, five of them are in college. Our son, Tom, is the oldest, married to Janie, with twins Katie and Lauren and Emily. They live in Columbia, Missouri. David is next, married to Marsha with Sam (our oldest grandchild), Brian and Kimmy. They lived for a while in Skaneateles, New York, near Syracuse. In August of 2008, they moved to Eden, Utah. Our youngest is Carol, married to Dave, and they have our youngest grandchildren, Jason and Jordan. Happily they live in St. Louis, nearby. We have a wonderful, caring family. I am writing this for all of them and for anyone else who might benefit.

Relating this account in chronological order is all

but impossible, but the overall progress of Gene's illness should be clear, as well as the difficulties that friends and family faced. However, there is hope for the future. The Alzheimer's Disease Research Center at Washington University in St. Louis is now looking into treatment that will halt the advance of Alzheimer's and also testing to see if they can find markers that will identify a person who will get the disease before it shows outward symptoms and then developing ways to prevent it. Much progress is being made.

Gene graduated from Washington University in 1954.

*Betty and Gene at their engagement party in 1954. Their daughter
Carol wore her mother's dress at her engagement party 33 years later.*

Above: Fort Belvoir, 1954. Gene is in the middle of the back row.

Below: Gene in Germany, 1955.

July 7, 1956

1

Our Life Before

When we got married after almost a four-year courtship (eighteen months of which Gene was in Germany), I had the theory that I should always get up when Gene did and prepare his breakfast. It really wasn't a hardship for me as I am a morning person and I had to wake Gene up anyway. One time when the alarm went off, he grabbed the clock and tried to flush it down the toilet. That's when I made the decision to wake him up myself.

As time went on, breakfast turned into just coffee and then it turned into "C & C", as in Cat and Coffee. I would go downstairs (we always lived in a two story house) and fix his coffee and then bring a cup of coffee up in one hand and the cat Smudgy in the other. Then the cat died and some years later Gene stopped drinking coffee.

Our three kids arrived in a timely fashion. Friends and family later referred to us as the "Leave It To Beaver" family. I take that as a compliment but maybe they thought we were dull!

Gene was active in coaching David's soccer teams

— which he admitted he knew nothing about — and his baseball teams, which he knew a lot about. Tom's teams always seemed to have coaches so he was just a spectator at those games.

Gene had coached in Germany when he was in the army. He also represented a soldier in a military trial. I think he was instrumental in winning that case. His gift for gab served him well.

He was also a Boy Scout merit badge counselor and did a lot of camping with the boys' troops. Both Tom and David are Eagle Scouts. Gene took their troop out to our farm to camp several times. One time our beagle, Angel (she wasn't) went with them. When the boys set up their tents and cook sites, Angel stole a whole pound of bacon right out of one of the coolers and ran off with it. All the boys learned a valuable lesson!

The Smith Family, Easter Sunday, 1968.

After he returned from Germany and two months before we got married, Gene started his career at Nooter Corporation, a steel plate fabricator, as a sales engineer. He had a passion for numbers and leadership. Whenever we visited his office, we were amazed at how neat his desk was and that was true at home as well. He was with Nooter for forty-one years and shepherded the company through good times and bad, rising to the office of President. He was instrumental in diversifying Nooter, which has stood them in good stead all these years. After his retirement and as long as he was able, we socialized with friends that he had made there through the years.

Gene was a do-it-yourself person. In our second house in Creve Coeur, I came home one night and found he had punched a hole in the wall in our bedroom. I was aghast! It had a peaked roof and he made a wonderful cozy study out of it, putting in a window and making a desk to fit against the wall. It had kneeholes and side drawers for each of us. We were to share the area; however, I soon took over the whole thing. I don't think he ever used his side. I loved that cozy room. Later, he paneled the basement and made it a wonderful gathering place. That was a family project. Tom and David helped with the paneling, and Carol and I painted the walls. The boys always said, "Give Dad a screwdriver and a hammer and he could do anything".

Gene experimented with wine making. I don't drink wine so I don't know whether it was good or not. He stored it downstairs and later found that some of the wine in the bottles had evaporated.

Years later we learned that Carol and her friends took out the corks and sipped a little from most of the bottles. (I thought I had such good kids but you never know!) The corks didn't fit tightly after that and the wine turned to vinegar.

When Tom was sixteen, he worked one summer as a lifeguard at Trout Lodge, the YMCA camp in Potosi, Missouri. He called one night wanting to take a quickie course to learn to scuba dive. Gene thought it was much too quick a course and scuba diving was not something one should take lightly. He suggested that when Tom came home and school started in the fall, he, Tom, and David should take a scuba diving course at the local high school. Tom was very disappointed and I know he thought it would never happen. However, it did. They had a ball learning scuba together. They ate a banana underwater, pulled

Gene at work at the farm.

off each other's masks, and simulated other disasters that might happen underwater, as well as studied together. For some years after that our vacations included a place where the three of them could scuba dive. A few years later, Carol took lessons with Dave, her boyfriend then and now her husband.

We went once to Galena, Illinois, to ski with our friends, the Haumessers, their daughter, Beth, and our daughter, Carol. Gene had skied in Germany, so he and Arnold Haumesser went down one of the difficult slopes. Beth and Carol were on a chair lift going up the slope as Gene and Arnold skied straight down, which is not the correct way! The ski patrol was blowing their whistles at them and people were staring at those two cowboys. Then Beth and Carol realized that those two cowboys were their dads! At the bottom of the slope Gene fell, and I think that's what later caused his hip pain.

We had many great trips as a family and with other families. Gene was a great fun–loving family man. During these perfect years, I felt God working to prepare me for the future. All around me friends and acquaintances were hav ing sicknesses or accidents. I wondered what our situation would be. I knew God would not give us more than we could handle and I knew He would help us through whatever was coming.

A bump in our road occurred in 1991 when I was diagnosed with breast cancer. I had a mastectomy a couple of weeks later. Gene was so very supportive and loving during that time. So sweet. I was lucky, since my lymph nodes were clear and I needed no further treatment. Thank you, God!

I was active at my church and belonged to a prayer group, which certainly helped me and gave me strength in good times and bad. Prayer is a powerful tool and Jesus gives you the strength you need.

Above: Sam, Jason, and Brian with Grandpa

Below: Kimmy, Katie, Lauren, and Grandpa

Carol and her dad at a Kappa Alpha Theta father's weekend at Mizzou.

Katie, Lauren, Grandma, Emily, Jason, Grandpa, Jason and Carol at the Transportation Museum in St. Louis

A family portrait, 40th Wedding Anniversary, 1996. Back row: Tom, Gene, Dave, Dave. Middle row: Janie, Betty, Jason and Carol, Marsha, Sam. Front row: Emily, Katie, Lauren, Brian, and Kimmy (Jordan in Carol's tummy.) At French Lick!

Gene's 70th birthday.

2

Beginnings

When did it start? What did we notice? How did it begin? I have never asked, "Why us?" Everyone has problems of some sort or another and actually up until this point we certainly had lived a charmed life. So why *not* us?

Have you ever been asked, "What is the Defining Moment in your life?" This is a hard question if you look at your whole life. However, it becomes easy as I look at this terrible disease that was evolving in one of us but was effecting both of us, as well as our family and friends. I can see five Defining Moments for Gene as well as for me:

First: The Houston incident

Second: The Nooter stockholders meeting

Third: Caregivers coming to the house

Fourth: Calling 911

Fifth: Using Hospice.

Maybe there were earlier signs. As we age, we do funny things. If you are under 60, it's just one of those things, a sort of brain freeze. However, if you are over 60, you think you are getting senile. Most of these happenings we just brush off. A case in point: One night Carol made some pesto with fresh basil from their yard. Dave had just planted some and she thought she knew where it was. She was so proud of her accomplishment, but the dish didn't taste right. When Dave asked her where she pickedthe basil, she showed him. Oh dear, it wasn't basil! How many of us do dumb things, but fortunately there are no witnesses and no consequences; so we never have to tell anyone. We all had a great laugh about Carol's pesto, especially her son Jason and her daughter Jordan. They checked to be sure the plant that Carol used was not poisonous. I can't imagine what they would have thought if I had done such a thing – probably never let me cook again. Maybe that's not a bad idea!

In 1993, when Gene was 60, he began having that universal aging problem of not finding the right words, names and places. We were concerned but not a lot. We knew everyone had this problem. However, for a man who was a big talker and always called everyone by name, this was a bigger sign than we thought. But what to do about it?

Around May of 1994, Gene had an appointment with Dr. Bill Phillips, an internist and cardiopulmonary specialist. Gene's previous doctor would not take our insurance and he decided he needed a checkup. He was concerned about his word loss and I was noticing more and more that he was substituting meaningless phrases to replace words he could not recall. All his tests were normal except for some allergies. He had quit smoking twenty years earlier and drank only socially. The doctor was concerned about his inability to find words, but there was nothing we could do about it except wait and watch.

I felt his writing skills were getting progressively worse. He never was a good speller. I'm not either — thank goodness for spell check! — but he was a fine writer. When he was in the army in 1954 and 1955 and stationed in Nuremberg, Germany, with the Corps of Engineers, he wrote long love letters to me that I still treasure. We were engaged at the time, and I usually got a letter every other week. Most were written over a week's time. He wrote of his experiences. His platoon went out on bivouac for two weeks at a time, fixing roads and bridges that had been damaged during World War II. Some of his letters were interrupted with pen in hand; the writing would just fall off as he fell asleep. As I look over these letters, I find them very informative and loving. I felt that I got to know another side of him. I waited each day to see if one arrived. (I kept his letters and he kept mine and I still have them all.) (Maybe I will write a book about Gene's experiences during the Cold War - 1955!)

Gene often wrote a poem for the birthday parties of good friends. He wrote one of his very best for our daughter's wedding in 1987. I thought it was very clever.

The Eight Year Courtship

1979 Dave called Carol one day in September
     (Sept. 14) Their first date they will always remember.

1980 Dave took off to the wild, wild west
     And Carol now knew that Dave was the best.

1981 A year from then, Dave's back again
     Saying, "I love you" at old Mizzou.

1982 Then one more year at old Mizzou
     But not so much, "I love you".

1983 Dave is a Junior and a big frat man
     Carol is a Sophomore and getting a tan.

1984 Dave's last year, their love is dear
     Theta potatoes and Lamb chops too
     Even thru this, their love was true.

1985 Carol graduates and heads for the South
     Dave lands a job and heads for the North
     It's now up to AT&T if love will spring forth.

1986 In '86 the battle raged between
     North and South
     Carol wondered if Dave would ever get
     the words out of his mouth.

1987 They met in KC for the final settee
     When the last gun was heard, Dave said,
     "Shut up, shut up, will you marry me?"

August 1 The Courtship is finally coming to a close
     We are all happy whom both of you chose.

So now we send you off with love, hope and rhyme
And raise our glasses to toast the greatest marriage
of all time.

                       To Dave and Carol with love

It distressed me terribly to think that a man who accomplished so much in his lifetime, becoming president, then chairman of the board at Nooter Corporation, a great conversationalist, and writing a poem like the one above, was now losing little by little all of that. On my morning walks, I talked with my two neighbors about some of the strange things that Gene did and they mostly listened. Sometimes they commented that their husbands did similar things, but I knew Gene was different.

Gene worked very hard to compensate for what he was losing. When we were on our way to a dinner party, he would ask me to go over the names of people we thought would be there. He would repeat them and then ask again and repeat them again. By the time we got to the party, I was worn out with this exercise. I kept telling him, that he should join the real world. Most of us just didn't call people by name, we said merely, "Hello, how are you?" and not their name in case we had it wrong or had a senior moment and couldn't even remember our best friend's name. But that wasn't my husband's way; he always called people he met by name and it really bothered him that he was having such trouble remembering. I tried to shield him or explain to others when he goofed up.

At a dinner party in the old days, Gene was usually the leader of the conversation, bringing up politics or other news items, sometimes being the devil's advocate just to make things interesting. There was never a lull in any conversation when Gene was around.

Then I noticed he was becoming more and more quiet, participating less, and sometimes joining the conversation with comments that had already been made, as if this were a new subject. Friends hadn't noticed he was having a problem and would jump on him with teasing comments like, "Where have you been?" and "Aren't you listening?" "Hey, are you sleeping?" I would cringe but didn't know what to do.

Because he could not think quickly or think of the right word right away, he was slow in speaking up. When he did get his thoughts together and tried to speak, he would get walked on, so he would remain quiet again. He knew this was happening and mentioned it to me, but I was at a loss as to how to counsel him.

As was his way, he would greet friends enthusiastically when we first arrived. When they realized that he wasn't contributing anything, they would talk among themselves, ignoring Gene. At one party at our house, he came out to the kitchen where I was getting the dinner ready and said, "No one is talking to me!" I tried to soothe him but he went into his study and pouted. At a dinner party at a friend's house, he got upset about being left out of the conversation, left the dining table, went into the living room, and put his feet with shoes on their glass top coffee table! I was mortified! I got him to take his shoes off and lie down on the couch. Another couple had driven us, so we couldn't just leave. Gene was more and more unhappy, it seemed. I knew I was losing him.

One time I was getting ready for a dinner party at our house, he suggested that maybe he could be more a part of the conversation at the table if he was not seated at his usual place at the end, so I started seating him in the middle or nearer to me. That helped for a short time. He tried so hard to find a way to be more involved in the conversations and I tried to direct the conversation toward him.

Some of our friends, seeing the changes, were still comfortable talking with him and I am forever grateful to them. After a while, he had only two subjects that he would talk about: a situation in the army when his jeep had tipped into the water and he had gotten into the water to save the driver; and working at Nooter. We often had a hard time figuring out what he was trying to tell us. I knew the story about the jeep, so I could enlighten his friends a little.

When Gene was telling a tale or talking about something that had happened and could not find a word, he would look at me and expect me to supply it. It was strange because about seventy-five percent of the time I did come up with the word that he was looking for. However, if I could not supply the right word he would get very angry. This was quite frustrating for both of us, and awkward for our friends, who had never seen Gene like this.

I cannot imagine the depth of his frustration, knowing this slide was happening. He continued to amaze me with his ability to face these problems and try to correct them or, at least, find a way to cope. I continued to try hard to give him all the encouragement I could.

3

Hearing Aids

Gene thought it might be possible that his ears were at fault. After testing, yes, he did have some hearing loss, and we hoped that hearing aids would eliminate the problem. If anything, they made it worse because he kept adjusting them and taking them out and of course they would squeal. I crawled under the table on two occasions when he dropped one and even drove him back to a country club after he had been at a business meeting. They had not vacuumed yet and luckily the hearing aid was on the floor. Another time a hearing aid just disappeared into thin air at a hotel room in Denver. We took all the bedding off, looked everywhere, even went back to the restaurant. We tried to backtrack all our steps and checked the car we had been driven in. The staff at the hotel was most helpful, searching our room, but to no avail. These hearing aids were expensive and had already been replaced when he lost both of them earlier. Time-wise, they were still under warranty, but only one replacement was allowed. (I still can't figure out what happened to that little hearing aid.)

The real problem, of course, was that he could not understand what people were saying, not that he couldn't hear them.

Then one day, Gene gave me the hearing aid and asked me to put in a new battery. By that time he was only using one because sometime before he had taken them out, put them on his desk and had bitten into one. I guess he thought it was candy. I assumed it was destroyed, but our technician glued it back together and it became Gene's favorite. I put it in a safe place, meaning to put the battery in when I had time; I didn't see the point in rushing. He never asked for it again. So that was the end of his hearing aids and I think it was a relief to both of us.

4

More Early Signs

Our sons were engineers like their dad. The three of them enjoyed this camaraderie. Later they would tell me that Dad just didn't make sense and sometimes I was a witness to that. For instance, the problem we had with the trees at our lake house. In 1987 we bought a house at TanTarA at Lake of the Ozarks in mid-Missouri. We had years of fun there. Pat and Arnold Haumesser were a part of our life there, as well as Pete and Corinne Leach and Duke and Margie Reisner, who all had their own places. We usually went when one of those couples were there. Pete and Gene had fun fishing and we all played tennis and golf. Lots of good food was had by all, either at one of our homes or at one of the great restaurants nearby. When the mall was built that added to our activities.

Gene wanted to see the lake from our deck; in the winter he could, but not in the summer. The trees had grown a lot since we bought the house. One summer he said all the trees between our home and the lake should be topped for about a half mile from our deck. We tried to explain to him that those trees belonged to other people. He didn't care. He wanted them cut, no matter the cost. He asked me to talk to all the people involved and tell them that we were going to have their trees topped. He was extremely adamant that this problem be taken care of. I found it interesting that he could remember that he wanted those trees cut down even when he couldn't remember other things. He also had an issue with the eaves of the porch, which needed to be painted by the roofer, but I couldn't seem to get that done. He became more angry about these things than was warranted. I decided that I wouldn't take him to the lake anymore. It was too much stress for me and probably for him also.

During the discussion about the trees and in other discussions, I noticed that Gene had tunnel vision. He sure had tunnel vision about the trees and the eaves! If he got on one subject and was going down a certain path, there was no way that anyone could reason with him or get him off that track. He was very single-minded. I always felt that if you were explaining something to someone and he or she didn't seem to understand, you could use another, similar situation to make your point. This had previously worked with Gene but not anymore. In fact, he would usually get extremely irritated.

In another instance we were talking with Tom about a home loan. I had no knowledge on this subject. Tom explained it very well and I felt I understood. Gene, however, was very confused and could not understand the concept at all. In fact he became very argumentative, and I realize now how frustrated he must have been. These episodes of confusion and anger were happening more and more often and we realized that it wasn't just his not finding the right word, but his not comprehending words or concepts as well. Silly me, I was beginning to think that I was getting smarter because I could understand things that Gene couldn't.

Early on there were times that he relayed information from an article that he had read in the newspaper. I had read the same piece and didn't think he had it right, but I considered that I could be wrong. In some cases I would go back and find the article. I discovered I was not wrong; he was. Other times I thought he was saying something incorrectly but I wasn't sure. It made me wonder if *I* was getting everything mixed up. I began to second-guess myself. At times I felt smarter than he was and then at other times I would doubt myself. Who is having the problem here?

Gene and his pontoon boat at Lake of the Ozarks.

5

Houston

A turning point in this "ride" was in November of 1996. This was the beginning of the Defining Moments, the first. We were in Houston on business with other couples from Nooter. When we arrived, one of his colleagues rented a car and we drove to the hotel. Gene had a luncheon meeting at one of their subsidiaries and left in the car by himself. He had been instrumental in buying this plant so he had been there many times but not recently. At about 3 P.M., one of the men called to say that Gene had not arrived for lunch. Knowing how bad the traffic was in Houston, we were afraid he might have had an accident, so one of the wives helped me call the traffic center and then the hospitals.

As we were doing this, Gene walked into our hotel room looking very forlorn and said, "There is something wrong with my brain!" We were so happy to see him, but my heart dropped when he said that. I answered, "I know!" We hugged each other and cried. This was a big turning point. Maybe it was a relief to admit to each other what each of us had secretly been suspecting. It was the beginning of a new life for us.

Yes, a Defining Moment. Gene explained that he had been driving around for several hours trying to find their office. He said he finally gave up and stopped for something to eat. Somehow, he found his way back to the hotel. I think that was a miracle.

After seeing Dr. Phillips, who recommended that we see a neurologist, we made contact with the Mayo Clinic in Minnesota and got an appointment for mid-January of 1997. Gene went through all the tests. The clinic is so well organized. When we checked in, they had all our appointments and tests arranged. We could go to our hotel room and never had to go outside. There was a lot of walking, which was not a problem for us.

Mayo is quite a maze but we learned it quickly. We were there five days. We also went to a movie and actually had a nice time, at least I did. But, of course, I was not being stuck with needles and having my body explored many times a day. We had nice dinners, met other patients we could chat with, discussed the doctors we had seen and wondered what the doctors would find. He was still able to communicate pretty well then.

Gene had every test possible that could tell the doctors something about his brain. It turned out that his brain was unique. On the left side was a big black area, which meant that those brain cells were atrophied or dead. The gray matter is the smart part of your brain and it looks gray on the MRI's. Gray is good, black is bad. There were white areas as well. What is white? I don't know!

We came away from our trip to Mayo not knowing much more than we did when we arrived. We received a very detailed report telling us what Gene did not have. No stroke, no tumor, no hardening of the arteries, no lack of air to the brain. Most of these things had been suggested to us as possibilities before we went to Mayo by helpful friends. The discharge diagnoses from Mayo stated, "Asymmetrical Cortical Degeneration Syndrome, Paretorfrontal-type of uncertain etiology." Now we knew! It was stumping the doctors as well as us.

They did agree that Gene had severe aphasia. The doctors at Mayo wondered why we were there when St. Louis has Washington University and one of the best Alzheimer's research centers in the world. They were not saying he had Alzheimer's, but that he did have a related dementia with a very long unpronounceable name. Dr. Leonard Berg was just retiring as head of the Alzheimer's Research Center at Washington University and Dr. John Morris was taking his place. Mayo suggested that we get into their program. Gene and I both thought this was an excellent idea.

6

Stockholder's Meeting

Now we come to the Second Defining Moment. After we got back from Mayo, it was time for the Nooter stockholder's meeting. Normally Gene led the meeting. Each year he would work diligently on his speech and coordinate it with George H. and George B. I would hear him practice and practice. For the past few years he'd had trouble with his everyday speech and would use meaningless phrases to replace words that he couldn't come up with. Years earlier he had been so hard on Carol because she interspersed her conversation with a lot of "uh"s. Of course, we all do that but he was not very tolerant. The years before when he asked me to listen to his speeches I would point out that he was using too many filler phrases. He was shocked. He tried so hard to correct that, but just could not find the right words or sometimes any words.

Now this year of 1997, before the meeting, he wanted to read me his speech. I was standing on the stairs halfway up, looking down at him.

He read this to me:

"Good morning. Normally, I would do most of the talking

Gene in his office at Nooter Corporation with an uncharacteristically messy desk.

at our stockholder's meeting, but today, George, Ross and Ray will need to cover for me.

"Therefore, I thought I should explain this to everyone.

"I went to my internist recently because I thought I had some medical problems. My internist told me that everything was fine but he thought I should go to a neurologist. The neurologist is pretty sure that I have a brain disorder – but all of the tests haven't come in yet. They think it is half Alzheimer's Disease and half Pick's Disease.

"I was going to retire at 65, but this being the case, I probably will retire a little sooner this year.

"That's all I can tell you right now, so I will turn the meeting back over to George."

Whew, what a speech and I truly cannot begin to explain my feelings. I couldn't say a word, just ran down the rest of the stairs and hugged him.

When we were at the management dinner that evening, I learned that when he delivered his speech at the stockholder's meeting that morning, he received a standing ovation and there was barely a dry eye in the house. Such a classy thing to do, and that was Gene. Truly honest, not hiding this big problem but meeting it head-on.

Gene was chosen to throw out the first pitch at a Cardinals baseball game in 1996 representing Nooter Corporation in celebration of their 100th anniversary. He loved the company and the employees loved him back.

7

Frustration

When Gene retired, he had to find something to do and turned to the Internet, which he had been using for years. His communication skills and comprehension were becoming worse, and I must say that it was a tense time at home. I could not reason with him, and he would become very frustrated because I was not doing what he wanted, usually something that was impossible for me to do anyway.

He used the computer to trade stocks, get quotes and research stocks. I actually became somewhat of an expert in working out computer problems for him but some things he wanted were beyond me. Thankfully his sister came to visit from Las Vegas and she was a self-taught computer guru.

One thing he wanted me to do was to fix the mouse so he had to click it only once. At that time, the mouse had to be clicked twice. I didn't have a clue how to do that and actually thought it couldn't be done. Lo and behold, his sister fixed it so he had to click it only once to get where he was going. Then he was angry at me because I hadn't done it.

After she went back home, I would call her and she would walk me through some problem I had. Gene was very, very angry if the computer didn't work the way he wanted it to and angry with me when I couldn't fix it. It didn't matter what I was doing, I had to fix his computer that moment. At times he became so agitated that I canceled everything I was doing that week to stay home and get him calmed down as well as myself. I must admit that I resented these interruptions to my life.

Gene thought he was doing something useful when he worked on his computer, although soon after he retired we both decided that he should turn our finances over to an advisor. He continued to watch and research the market. He gave me some ideas for my stock club. Sometimes I asked him to look up a stock for me. He was happy to do that. It was amazing how much he worked on the computer. It kept him very busy, and when we had friends over he would show them what he could do. Many did not use a computer, so they marveled at his skill and that made him feel really good.

Earlier he had gotten into trading stocks with just a little money and ended up with a very respectable portfolio. But now he was losing the ability to make good decisions. After he gave up actually trading stocks he made fake portfolios. He had piles of them printed out. Then, little by little, he lost all of his ability to work on the computer. It was heartbreaking to see him sitting in his chair at the computer trying to do what he used to do and giving up. Then he would look out the window for a while. We had bird feeders that he could see from his window, and watching the birds helped his emotional equilibrium and gave him something to do.

During the time he could still work on the computer–and he did consider it his work—he printed out information about each stock and put the information from the printout back into the computer and printed it again. Many times he proudly showed me the paper he'd just printed out. He had three stacks of these papers on his desk, each about 10" high. One day while cleaning up I asked him if we could throw away some of these piles of papers. I thought he understood what I was saying and he said. "yes." I put them on a side table just in case he changed his mind. Several weeks went by and I figured it was safe to throw them out. A few days later, he was looking all over for those papers; Oh my, what a crisis. However, I was lucky. I hadn't put the trash out yet and they were all in the can and not even messed up! Was someone watching over me?

I truly believe that Gene's work on the computer kept his disease at bay for some time. Experts say, "Use your brain," and he certainly worked at it. Soon after he accepted the fact that he had a problem, he wanted to relearn how to use a simple calculator. He asked me to show him and he was so eager to learn but could not.

Before, this was a man who did not even need a calculator; he could do all that figuring in his head. When we talked about finances or anything to do with numbers, he rattled off all the numbers so fast, I had to stop him so I could write them down. His inability to comprehend how to use a calculator was a shock to me. It made me realize how much he had lost. I just can't imagine how he must have felt as each thing that he could do so easily became something that he could not do at all.

Gene wanted to be helpful, but there wasn't much he could do anymore. For a while he was very proud that he could help by cleaning up the kitchen each evening. It was a big help to me until the time came when he was getting water all over the kitchen floor and making a bigger mess. Then he started forgetting to do the dishes until it was time for us to go to bed. I then decided I would do the dishes right after dinner. It was taking him longer and longer to eat and I eat really fast, so I started cleaning up so that I was still in the kitchen with him. I hated taking over this one job of his but I sensed that he really did not want to do it anymore since he kept putting it off.

Another situation that we had to adjust too soon became obvious. He had been president of the Nooter Corporation in St. Louis (they didn't call them CEO's at that time). He had worked there for forty-one years and for many years he was second or third in command and then president, retiring as chairman of the board. He was used to giving orders, not taking them. Now suddenly, he was at home, losing some of his gray matter and being told what to do by his wife! He found he could not make decisions and could not fix things the way he used to. This was very hard for him to accept and it showed.

He had always been an excellent driver; one of the best drivers I ever rode with. Then he began doing dumb things, little misses, no big deal. He started cutting people off and driving down a street the wrong way. I began directing him more, and he was actually surprisingly directable.

When we drove out of town, I would map out the route and direct him. When we got into a city, I would watch the road signs and tell him which lane to get into and so forth. It seemed strange to me that he wasn't reading the highway signs and would not change lanes until I told him to, but at this point he followed my directions perfectly — we made a good team. I guess out of necessity I became a "backseat driver" sitting in the front. Finally it became easier for me to drive and I think he was glad. We were now living life on a downhill slope. This behavior was so different from his earlier years of looking at a map of our travel plans for the day, memorizing all turns, and not even referring to the map again.

In March of 2001, he needed his driver's license renewed. Dr. Phillips and Dr. Morris were both questioning whether he should drive at all. Gene didn't want to give up that freedom and I sure wished he didn't have to. We decided that he would drive only to those places that he was very familiar with. I hated the idea of taking his car keys away, but I knew that day was coming all too quickly. God stepped in again and I was saved that task. When we went to renew his license, he couldn't identify the signs: stop, yield, railroad crossing, and so forth. The woman giving the test was very kind and understanding and tested him several times, but he couldn't understand how to look into the machine.

He took a cheat sheet home of all the signs and signals. He worked very hard at finding the right words and then identifying each sign. I tried to help him remember the signs, but I knew he couldn't do it, and when we went back, sure enough he couldn't. My heart went out to him, but I knew this was a blessing in disguise. Gene was angry when we left that office but he cooled off quickly. This was another milestone. We were reaching for a goal that we didn't want to reach, but it was inevitable. We just didn't know how long it would take.

God has a plan for our lives if we believe in Him. I certainly felt that God was standing by us during all these years. I was thankful that Gene's license needed renewing at this time – it was so much easier and less emotional than my having to take his car keys away.

We continued to go to Rams football games downtown. Gene usually held the back of my hood to keep from getting lost in the crowds, which worked very well. Once we got separated at the escalator and that was very scary. He had been right behind me when I got on the escalator or so I thought, but when I got halfway to the bottom, I realized he was not behind me. I tried to stay calm; I could not go back up because all the escalators were going down at the end of the game. He did not have a cell phone and I didn't either. We had come down on the group bus and I was sure he would not know how to find it.

To my amazement just as I was trying to puzzle out what to do and praying, he was coming down the escalator! What a relief!! I thanked God for keeping him safe and answering my prayer. I think he was glad to see me. He seemed to enjoy the games, but I don't think he followed the plays or knew which side was which. If I cheered, he cheered. Many times it was a bit nerve wracking for me and maybe for him too, especially when he had to use the restroom.

Then one Sunday, as I was getting his clothes out to wear to the football game, he made it plain that he was not going. I was not sure he knew where we were going, and I must say, I had a fit! Unfortunately, I hate to change any plans at the last minute. I called a friend, who I knew loved going to the game and asked if she could go. I decided Gene could just stay home. I was mad! (I think I may have had my priorities mixed up.)

As I was ready to leave, he decided he wanted to go, but I said, "No." This time I think he was smarter than I was; it was time for him to stop going to the games.

8

Washington University

After returning from the Mayo Clinic we made an appointment with Dr. John C. Morris at Washington University's Alzheimer's Research Center. Gene became part of his study: the Memory and Aging Project. We knew that this was not designed to help us as much as to help future generations. Gene understood that and wanted to help others.

Dr. Morris subsequently became Gene's neurologist as well, so we saw him twice a year. We were kept abreast of the progress of the drug Aricept through the pipeline and when it became available, Dr. Morris prescribed it. Then a few years later, a related drug, Namenda, became available and Gene was given that. These drugs slow down the disease and were the best available at the time. Our visits with Dr. Morris were very helpful, as he explained what was happening very well. As the symptoms increased, Dr. Morris diagnosed Gene with atypical Alzheimer's Disease.

Gene also became part of a study of the brain by submitting himself to many MRIs. It turned out that his case history was so fascinating and unusual that Dr. Randy Buckner, a neuroscientist, presented his findings at a medical seminar in Stockholm, Sweden. Gene got a kick out of having a famous brain. We were given a huge poster with views of his brain and commentary about his case history. (see page 121)

I also became part of a study of caregivers. At that time, I was a caregiver of sorts, but nothing like I became later. I think back to what I said then. We have a video of another caregiver and myself that was used for the study, but for some reason I cannot talk myself into watching that video. This other caregiver's wife had Alzheimer's, and their journey was much farther along than mine at that time. Now I realize how naïve I was and how much I have learned since then. Having a deep faith in God and prayer has pulled me along this long road. Friends say that I look at a cup as half full rather than it being half empty. I guess I do. I try not to complain and to stay positive. I really thank all my friends who have listened to me as I have used them as a sounding board and I thank each of them for their support, prayers, and advice. As the Girl Scout song says, "Make new friends and keep the old, one is silver and the other gold." This is so true.

Several tests are used at the Memory and Aging Center at Washington University to determine the progression of the disease. One test is the Mini-Mental State which is graded from 30 to 0 with 30 being the best.

Normal people score 30.

In 1998, the first time he was tested, Gene came up with a score of 19.

In 2001, the score was 10.

In 2003, it was 3.

In 2005, the score was again 3.

However, on the last visit, 2006, it was zero, because they were unable to test him. He could not follow directions of any kind. He could not find any words and could not understand them either.

Another test was called the Boston Naming Test with the best score being 15.

In 1998, his score was 9.

In 2001, it was down to 4.

In 2002 and 2003, it was 2.

In tests at Mayo, he had trouble repeating a sequence of four digits or a list of four words.

During the early years, Gene had a problem with using the wrong word, had problems with spelling, writing and doing math problems. He couldn't concentrate or remember immediate information. When we asked him a question that could usually be answered with a simple yes or no, he would go into a long dissertation on what he thought the subject was, a lot of which did not make sense to us, and he made up words to fill in his sentences.

9

More Changes

Gene always loved to garden. He loved to re-plant and trim plants. I frequently said that his mother never let him make mud pies, because he was so happy making a hole and stirring around in all that mud with his hands. One day I watched as he trimmed one of our ornamental fruit trees in the backyard. For several days he trimmed it back, each day a little more. I got concerned and suggested that maybe he had trimmed enough. His reply was rather angry. He said he knew what he was doing.

A workman had been there for several days repair-ing some termite damage in the bay window in Gene's study. During that time Gene had talked to him in his way and had showed him some pictures of the vessels Nooter had built. Of course it was obvious that Gene had a problem. (Whenever I had a workman in the house I told them first thing that Gene had a dementia problem so that they would understand if Gene stood and watched them or tried to talk to them.) Well, after several days of trimming, the tree was now only one stick! All the branches were gone. Gene wanted me to ask this work-man to cut the rest down. I said I could not do that because that was not the reason he was here. However, the next morning I showed the workman the stump. I had earlier showed him the progress of the trimming. I mentioned that Gene had asked me to have him cut down the rest of the stump. It was only about three feet high by now. Bless him, he said he would. He had only a little work left to do at our house, but said he would come back after he finished at his next job later that day. My goodness, I did not want him to do that and tried to talk him out of it but he insisted and sure enough he arrived around 5:30 P.M. I was appalled that he did not have a power saw and had to use our little handsaw. It took him some time, but he finally got it cut at ground level. Gene was so happy. The workman said that if I ever needed him to please call him and left his card. He refused any payment.

This whole episode was a roller coaster of emotions for me. First, I was upset at Gene for "trimming the tree," sad that Gene did not understand what he was doing, glad that Gene had someone to talk to, and touched that this man was so kind and thoughtful. As I write this, tears come to my eyes. We were blessed with many who showed extraordinary kindness to us through our long journey

Some years back when he was answering a questionnaire, Gene wrote that gardening was his favorite hobby; now he couldn't do it at all. I think he knew he had gone too far with that poor little ornamental tree. Now when someone asked him what he was doing in the yard, expecting to hear Gene's elaborate plans, he said, "That's Betty's job." I was not a gardener but I tried and soon realized that it was not my thing. It was another moment of sad realization. This deterioration of all the things he enjoyed was so hard to watch. And he knew it was happening.

Some of his other loves were golf and tennis. We were not good golfers, but we had a lot of fun for a while. Then things got a little tense. Driving the golf cart became a problem. Normal golf manners were ignored. One day when we were playing alone at TanTarA, I watched him swing and swing and miss the ball completely. Each miss was a tug at my heart. I suggested that it was time to give up golf. No comment from Gene. Then the next morning, he announced that he had decided not to play golf any more. All his idea! And thus he was in control.

We loved golf

and tennis

Tennis became a real sore point with the men he played with. He became very argumentative and unpleasant on the court. A player from one group called to tell me he was no longer a part of the group. Just like that! I was more than angry. I wished they had given me some time to think about it so I could have made up some excuse without telling Gene that they had kicked him out of the group.

I quickly thought of a solution and asked his chiropractor, or Dr. Marc Hubbard—we saw him every week because the treatment helped Gene's sciatica—to suggest to Gene that twice a week was too much tennis and maybe he should cut out one game. As we left the office, I suggested that he cut out that particular game. Gene thought that made sense so we got that problem solved. I am still hurt by the way this group handled Gene. I had not realized how disruptive he had become on the court, but some warning would have helped.

The other tennis group (good friends from Nooter) was more classy and thoughtful. They told me that they would let him play for the rest of the season which was only a few more weeks, but I decided that I should put them out of their misery. (I also played tennis and when I realized how disruptive Gene had become, I knew it was not much fun to play with him.) I made up some tale, so that Gene would not play anymore. I found telling him little white lies was a necessity and perfectly acceptable. Then the group told him they were quitting a little earlier at the end of the season because of guys traveling. Now he had given up all his tennis.

I knew he needed exercise. We went to Wellbridge to water walk about once or twice a week. This activity helped his back and I also did exercises in the water. First we had a trainer, but Gene had trouble following her so I copied some of her easier moves and he followed me. We did a simple routine and he seemed to enjoy this activity. It was close to Duffy's restaurant (see *Duffy's* chapter, page 68) and that was a great reward for both of us after our workout plus no cooking for me.

As the year went by he took more and more time to get ready for the pool. I started beating him in. I would begin my water walking and he would join me. When we got out, I would get dressed and usually find him waiting for me. Then I began waiting for him and eventually had to send someone into the men's dressing room to see what was holding him up. These outings were getting increasingly stressful for both of us.

You've heard the story of the Emperor's New Clothes.

That is what I named this episode. One day (I even remember that it was a Tuesday, it was that awful) I was in the pool with more women than usual. All of a sudden I heard one of the women calling my name. I looked up and saw Gene holding his towel over his arm and standing in his birthday suit! I rushed out of the pool and kept trying to get him to hold the towel in front of him and direct him back into the men's locker room, but he just stood there. He was completely unaware. Finally an attendant came out and took him into the men's locker room. Soon he came out with his swimsuit on; he had no idea that anything had been wrong. It really was kind of funny and all the women were very understanding.

I hated to give up the water walking, but I couldn't see how we could manage to continue. The family bathroom was across the hall from the men's locker room. Even if I got him dressed there, he would still have to walk through the men's locker room and I would have to go through the women's locker room. I was afraid that walking through the locker room by himself would be confusing and maybe he would take off his swimsuit and come out as he had before. I figured we would have the same problem if he dressed at home. So that ended that activity.

10

Friends

Our life reminded me of a beach slowly being washed away. But I still looked for the positive. I tried not to complain, but talking with my family and friends was great therapy for me. I urge anyone who is going through anything like this: Talk, talk, talk. Get it out but don't complain. Try to make the episodes funny. Give the facts, even ask for suggestions. Most people like to be asked for suggestions. But first use prayer and ask God to guide you.

During these weeks, months and years, many people would show their sympathy and support in different ways. Our friends were a wonderful comfort. We had friends who traveled with us and continued to do so: Spain, the Rhine River, Russia, Alaska, Puerto Vallarta, and the Dominican Republic. I certainly appreciated their companionship and tolerance. It was very hard for me to travel alone with Gene when he had no one to talk to. Most of the overseas trips occurred before 2002 and traveling got progressively harder. He was pretty agreeable on the Russian trip in 2002 because we were with the Reisners and our good friend Janet Hays and they made him feel comfortable.

Four special couples were a constant support to us during these years and we did a lot of traveling with them. However two of the wives, Margie and Corinne, were diagnosed with pancreatic cancer within a few months of each other. They had different doctors, different treatment, went to different hospitals and they each passed away a few months apart. Their illnesses lasted two years. Gene and I visited with them or went places with them when they were able. He knew they were ill and was very concerned and sympathetic. I am not sure how much he understood but he did know something was drastically wrong.

The third couple I call the Energizer Bunnies—Pat and Arnold Haumesser. I'm not sure I could have coped through these years without their continued support. At 4:30 some days the phone would ring. It was Pat: "Arnold is grilling some hamburgers, nothing fancy, but can you join us for dinner?" They knew that a hamburger would make Gene happy. Those were special times! They always felt comfortable having us over for dinner, even when we were not sure how Gene would react. He did love hamburgers so that always worked. At first we tried playing bridge—Arnold was just learning—but Gene couldn't get the concept of playing from the dummy when he got the bid. He had been an excellent bridge player and now he couldn't do it.

Friends are so important but you can't just sit back

Above: Arnold, Corinne, Pete, Margie, Betty, Duke, Pat, and Gene.

Below: Jerroy and Dodie Frank with us.

and wait for your friends to reach out to you; it's a two-way street. I find also that there is a time to accept help and be gracious about asking for help. Many friends you cannot repay in a million years, but you can be a friend to someone else who needs encouragement and support at a later time. Call your friends and family. Keep in contact with everyone you know, but don't complain.

Above: Bob and D'Arcy Elsperman with us at Lake of the Ozarks. D'Arcy was a great listening friend.

Gene found a special friend on the Disney Cruise with all our family.

11

Routines

Our new life together began to develop into a pattern. Slowly I began to take over one aspect of our life and then another. Gene was amazingly accepting of many of my suggestions. He seemed to want to help his situation as best he could and was good about listening to my ideas.

As we struggled with this progressive disease, we developed routines for almost everything. Thankfully, Gene was a very neat person and always put things away, unlike myself. He had a good sense about which shirts went with which pants and hung everything up or put it in the hamper right away after taking it off.

At some point I had to take over tieing his tie. That was certainly interesting; my son-in-law showed me how. I guess Gene taught the boys because I did not know how, although I am not sure the boys wore ties very often.

As time went on, if we kept to the routine, he was very self-sufficient. He continued to work at the computer as if he were going to a job. At bedtime, he kept to the routine, undressing in a certain order, putting his clothing in a certain place, brushing his teeth and taking pills. Gradually each task became too hard and I had to help. I began to put his clothes out for the day. Next I put toothpaste on his toothbrush and got his pills out. Later I had to check to see if he was using soap when he showered.

We were the generation that ate everything on our plates so eating was not a problem for a long time. Gene was never picky, although if he didn't like something, he would gently let me know. Then his eating habits changed, and I knew things were going downhill. When I called him in for dinner, he would look at his plate and say a big loud "No." (It was one of the few words he could still say.) I would leave his plate on the table, start eating myself, and pretty soon he would join me. I tried to fix meals I knew he liked. Then he seemed to forget that he did not like certain things and started eating everything without hesitation.

12
Duffy's

D uffy's is a sports bar not too far from where we live. It has the best hamburgers in town. At least that is what Gene thought. He liked, rather loved, their bacon cheeseburger. When we went somewhere else, he was never really satisfied, with the exception of the cheeseburger at McDonald's.

One year on my charge statement, I saw that we had been to Duffy's fifty-two times in that year. That is once a week, and I must admit I got tired of going there. However, I knew a trip there would make Gene very happy. Around four or five o'clock, he would come in and say "hamburger" or something similar, so that I knew that he wanted to go to Duffy's. If I had already started dinner, I would just put it all away for the next day and off we would go to Duffy's. He would finish his hamburger and fries and say, "That was good!" It was nice that he could enjoy this outing.

If someone else went with us, I always warned them to keep their fries on the other side away from Gene. Even when he still had fries on his plate he would take some of their fries if they were close.

Because we were there so often, one of the waitresses in particular would recognize us. By the time we were seated, she had a glass of red wine at his place and a glass of iced tea for me. They took my order quickly—they knew what Gene wanted—and we were served quickly. We went early so Gene wouldn't have to wait.

We went to Duffy's when Dave or Tom and their families were in town for family dinners and birthdays. Many times we met friends there. Once we had a new waitress and I forgot to say "bacon cheeseburger" or maybe she didn't catch it. When she brought Gene a plain hamburger, he knew something was different but couldn't make me understand the problem. He didn't make a scene but he was most unhappy. I didn't notice that the hamburger was naked. Something finally clicked but it was too late. I was upset with myself and felt sorry for Gene. When something like this happened I would continue to puzzle it out. I was thankful that I figured this one out so I could be sure not to make the same mistake again.

Eventually hamburgers became too hard for him to manage. The bun would slide off the meat and he didn't know what to do with it. Gene liked pizza too, so we switched to a bacon sausage pizza which was easier for him to manage. That worked for awhile.

Then he started having trouble sitting down. It was especially hard having him sit in a booth, something we had preferred. He could not get the concept of sliding into a booth. Once he tried to sit on the table. That was the last time we tried a booth, and soon our visits there ended as well.

I felt so badly when he couldn't go to Duffy's anymore but thankfully McDonald's still worked. When he could not ask to go out anymore and we were having a difficult day, I would suggest we go get a hamburger. He would brighten up and be very happy.

13

Wednesday Club

In November of 2002, I was thrilled to be asked to be the vice-president and president-elect of the Wednesday Club of St. Louis. It was a four-year commitment. This club was founded in 1890, one hundred and twenty years ago. It is an extremely well run, organized group of two hundred and seventy-five women. We meet every Wednesday from October through June, with a morning program at 11:00 A.M., an afternoon program at 1:15 P.M. and lunch in between. Usually around a hundred and twenty women attend each week. Our programs vary: music, science, literature, international relations, drama, education, history, poetics, civics, and creative works. The speakers presenting these programs are from the area universities and medical schools as well as others who are experts in their subject. We never have a bad program.

This was a big decision for me. Could I give enough time to the Wednesday Club and still give a lot of time to Gene? He could still stay home by himself and was still working on the computer most of the day. I asked him if he would mind (I had always asked him when I took a big job; like chairing the Shining Light Christmas Tree Lot or being president of several other organizations. He, of course, always said, "Yes"). However, this time I felt I was being a bit disingenuous and hypocritical because I figured he did not know what I was talking about. He did agree and I decided this was something I really wanted to do and so I told them, "Yes."

I knew it would take a lot of time, but we had an excellent staff, headed by our very capable Executive Director, Connie Ward. I also knew they would give me all the support I needed. As it turned out, I became acting president as well as vice president because the president was diagnosed with cancer and so I took over her job as well. Those four years kept me sane and I enjoyed them. It allowed me to be focused on something other than my problems, and everyone at the Wednesday Club was supportive and helpful. I know that I was a better caregiver because I had another outlet. I do encourage other caregivers not to give up their lives completely. Those years certainly help me now as I go forward.

One incident stands out during those four years. I had decided to hold the December board meeting at my home. I love to entertain and my house was all decorated for Christmas. The board consisted of twenty-eight members and of course, a few couldn't come. I usually had thirty-five at Thanksgiving for a sit-down dinner so under thirty was a breeze.

One of the caterers who worked at the Wednesday Club was coming to help. I had made some kind of casserole, salad, and dessert and all was ready. I had even typed out my agenda for the meeting, which would be held before lunch. Gene was usually okay with my entertaining. He just worked on his computer, and I think enjoyed seeing people in our house. Sometimes he would even come into the family room and do a little dance.

That morning as he was getting dressed with my help, he suddenly collapsed, falling slowly to the bathroom floor. He got up quickly and collapsed again. I got him into the bedroom to sit on the bed but he wanted to get up. But each time he did, he would collapse again. I had a terrible time keeping him on the floor so he wouldn't hurt himself or me as I tried to catch him each time. I called 911 and they came immediately.

I called Connie, the executive director at the Wednesday Club, and she called Lionelle, my vice-president. They came over as quickly as possible. As Gene was leaving in the ambulance and I was following behind in my car, I waved to the astonished members arriving for the meeting.

This collapse had happened once before while we were at the chiropractor's. Dr. Morris cut back on his Aricept for a while then and this time, too. The first time was right before this past Christmas and they kept him at the hospital. I had to stay all night because he didn't understand what was happening and the nurses would not have known what he needed. It was pretty much a sleepless night for me, but not a serious episode for Gene.

When I came home hours later from this last episode, everyone had left except Karen, the caterer, and the house was all cleaned up. She had waited for me to come home, so sweet of her. When I talked with Connie, who became such a good friend and confidant during those four years, she said all had gone so well. The food was good, the meeting was run well, and I was hardly missed! Lionelle had taken over admirably.

As my term came to an end, I decided I would start writing a memoir about Gene's journey. The Wednesday Club has a monthly writers' group and I figured it would be a good place to help me launch my thoughts. They were very supportive and encouraging. I read short excerpts at many of our meetings. They inspired me to keep going.

14

Gracie

About this time, I volunteered to keep Carol and Dave's yellow lab, Gracie, while they were on vacation. We had had many dogs through our married life: Jill, Lady, Mr. Sid and Angel, as well as two cats, Sugar and Smudge. Gene loved them all. But after Smudge, he was adamant that we shouldn't get another animal. Our kids thought that he should have one, so I mentioned it after Tom and Janie had visited. I said, "You know they just might bring us a puppy one of these days." Gene said, "Then they will have three." I was amazed that he remembered that they had two other dogs and could still make such a clever comment.

He had always loved Gracie and even when he could not remember most names, he remembered Gracie and talked to her a lot. Then I noticed he was paying less and less attention to her when we visited Carol and Dave. He even was becoming a little aggravated with animals. So when Carol brought Gracie over, he was not happy. He didn't want her to stay. After Carol left, he was most upset and ignored Gracie. I never really knew what he was thinking; maybe he was thinking that now Gracie was ours. I tried to tell him we were helping Carol out and that they would only be gone for a week.

Gracie always loved Gene and that day and for the rest of her stay with us, she sat by his chair whenever he was in his study, which was most of the time. I think he kind of liked her there except when he wanted to get up and she didn't move.

One afternoon Gracie started barking as I heard the front door close. It was unusual for Gene to venture outside on his own, but it was a beautiful day and maybe he couldn't resist. I quickly got the leash on Gracie and went out the back door. I wasn't in a rush. I figured Gene would just wander around the house. He didn't walk far or fast because his hip always hurt.

Gracie and I walked all around the house. No Gene. I looked up the street. No Gene. I then guessed he had gone back into the house, so I looked all over for him in the house. No Gene. Back outside, still no Gene. Now I was getting really worried and almost panicky. Should I drive around and look for him? Where to drive? I decided it was serious enough to call 911, which is patched into our community police department. I said my husband, Gene Smith, had walked out the door and I couldn't find him.

To my great relief, they said he was two blocks over. A man had spotted him walking down his street and felt that something was wrong. The man went out to talk to Gene, and of course, Gene could not talk, although I think he told the man his name. The man called the police and I arrived shortly thereafter. It was really scary.

Gene looked sheepish, scared, and relieved to see me. He quickly got into the car while I talked to the police and the Good Samaritan. The mystery remains as to how he walked so far so fast. His hip always hurt, even for short distances. I don't think he walked through the yards and walking up our street couldn't have been easy. And he would have had to walk along Clayton Road, which is a fairly busy thoroughfare with no sidewalks. I just can't imagine how he did it. I thanked God for taking care of him.

And I thanked Gracie for alerting me, but obviously I did not move fast enough. Maybe she barked because he had not taken her with him, but I think she was concerned about him and was watching out for him.

15

Skaneateles

In March of 2005, we had our kitchen redone. In planning this, I decided that while the new floors were being laid, we would go up to Skaneateles, New York, where our son David and his family lived. We were also having tile put on the entry floor, so we needed to get out of the house. All the activity would be too much of an interruption for Gene. Our granddaughter, Kimmy, was visiting us during her winter break. She was very good with her grandpa and tried to talk to him frequently. She flew with us to her home in Skaneateles and was a big help. We got a wheelchair in Cleveland, where we changed planes, and all went very smoothly.

However, after our daughter-in-law Marsha picked us up at the airport and we were about thirty-five minutes into our forty-five minute drive, I realized that we three girls had been talking mile a minute and ignored Gene. I reached over from the back seat (we always let him sit in the front seat) and patted him on the shoulder; and asked him how he was doing. I got a great loud "NOOO" for an answer and then he would not say anything else. Of course, he could not express what was bothering him and this was the root of his frustrations, which he acted out in many different ways. When we got to David's, it was dark, which I guess added to his confusion, and he would not get out of the car. Dave finally coaxed him out but he became quite agitated, yelling at Kimmy and me. Dave had to hold him in a bear hug because he was threatening me. It was a good thing that Dave was so strong.

Gene finally calmed down and I got him to bed that evening with no problem, but he started all over again in the morning. He did not know where we were and I am not sure he recognized David. Of course, he could not tell us what the matter was. We were in David's new house and maybe he thought our kitchen project had morphed into a whole new house. Dave again calmed him down. Our grandson, Brian, fixed Kimmy's computer so that Gene could get to his favorite and only web site that he used at home to work on his stocks. The printer didn't work the same and the fonts were different so he did not like it very much, but he seemed to know we were trying to help him. He kept asking when we were going home.

He was so agitated the night we arrived and the next morning that I called Dr. Phillips in St. Louis and described the situation. He called a nearby pharmacy so that we could get a medicine that would calm him down. Evidently New York has very strict laws about prescriptions and so our doctor had to fax them information to prove that he was a bona fide doctor. This was another frustration and it took some time.

Bless David! He offered to take his dad to the Nucor plant, where he was the general manager. Gene always liked to tour the steel mills where David worked. Of course, I worried about how they would handle Gene. It reminded me of getting a baby sitter for the kids and worrying about how they would do. Gene's day went well. David even got him a Nucor jacket, which he needed and enjoyed wearing.

Later when we drove around in the Village of Skaneateles, Gene actually recognized two places where we had stayed on other visits, as well as David's old house. When we had arrived the day before, it was dark and with the new house, Gene must have been totally confused and disoriented. The next day we drove to Binghamton to visit our eldest grandson, Sam, who was a freshman at the University there. Gene seemed to enjoy that trip and was not a problem.

I was a bit apprehensive about the trip back to St. Louis, but Gene was fine. David took us to the airport and lingered as we went through security. I could see the worry on his face. I had given Gene a tranquilizer but I'm not sure he needed it. The whole time we were in Skaneateles — only four nights — Gene had wanted to go home, so maybe he understood that now we *were* going home.

When we got home, our house was pretty torn up. The refrigerator was in his study, cooking and washing dishes had to be done at the bar, and we ate meals in the family room in front of the TV. However, mission accomplished, our floors were finished and beautiful. The work on the kitchen was progressing nicely.

16

Caregivers

The children had been after me to get someone to stay with Gene so I could have a break now and then. I was still leaving him by himself while I did short errands or taking him with me on others. I thought it would be a good time to start getting someone to come in when we came home from Skaneateles because the caregiver would seem to be a part of the construction crew who was a week into a four-week project of remodeling the kitchen. I didn't know how Gene would react to me leaving him all of a sudden with a stranger. I hoped this would be a good solution.

I had some leads but two people I called could not adjust their schedule to mine. However the third agency had what turned out to be the absolutely perfect person for us. My daughter-in-law's mother knew of a nun who, after fifty years, decided to leave her order in 1997. She set up an agency for caregivers called The Companion Network. God was truly looking down on us. This was the Third Defining Moment.

The person who came through the agency was Floss, and she became our guardian angel. She was wonderful with Gene and became my confidant. When I came home from being away, she would give me a complete report. (Again I remembered the days when the kids were small and I used a baby sitter.) It was wonderful and therapeutic for me to talk to her about Gene since she had firsthand knowledge of what he was doing. She had many good suggestions on how to handle him, helped me cope with the situations I encountered.

When Floss began to come to our home, during the kitchen renovation in March of 2005, she came three times a week, when I had meetings or a bridge game or a luncheon. With the construction going on in our house, Gene could no longer get his sandwich or Coke out of the refrigerator. He still spent a lot of time on the computer and Floss became an expert in getting it back to where he needed it to be. Gradually she came more often. Her many activities included fixing his lunch, talking with him if he wanted to try to talk, and taking him outside. She tried to get him to water the flowers, but mostly he would pick up leaves and sticks in the yard and driveway, usually one leaf at a time. His desire for neatness still showed. Floss liked to keep busy, so she always brought a book with her, but I doubt that she ever read any of it. When she was outside with Gene she would do some gardening or planting while Gene wandered around the yard. When I came home from one of my trips before Easter, she had planted flowers all around. Easter morning was like an Easter egg hunt as I wandered around the yard discovering a flower here and a flower there. What a sweet, sweet thing to do. She even brought me flowers in a fancy vase for my birthday, knowing that Gene couldn't do anything and wouldn't even remember it was my birthday. I was so touched.

Gene had always been very careful to keep the bird feeders full and he did not want water in the birdbath. With water standing, it made the birdbath dirty and he did not like that, so he swished out the water. He also kept it painted blue. The caregivers eventually took over the care of the bird feeders, but he continued to wipe water out of the birdbath.

The kitchen project was finished in record time. Amazingly, Gene realized it was ending and tried to ask Floss how much longer she was going to come—or at least that's what we thought he was trying to find out. She wasn't sure if he wanted her to come or not. I think he wanted her to come! They certainly got along well, and he got a lot more attention from her than I probably would have given him.

Floss spoiled me during her two years with Gene. When she arrived she would immediately start any wash I had and did any cooking I needed. She wrapped all my Christmas gifts and helped me get ready for luncheons and dinner parties. I still entertained a lot to keep Gene involved and our friends intact. She didn't hover over

Gene, but she was always in sight and able to help him with whatever he wanted. As I said earlier, she wanted to keep busy and found ways to do so.

17

Practice Trips

Eventually my kids felt that I should get away for a long weekend. I agreed and planned a get-away to our home at TanTarA with my bridge group that June. This was to be a sort of practice time away as I was planning to go to Germany the next April to see my grandson, Brian, with his parents, Marsha and Dave and sister, Kimmy. The Companion Network set up a schedule with Floss as the main caregiver and her brother-in-law Bill would stay with Gene at night. I did have other caregivers (who were very capable and wonderful) when Floss wasn't available, and they were used a lot when I went on "Practice trips."

I wrote down Gene's routine minutely, from the moment he got up in the morning until he went to bed at night. His schedule was very important and I tried to cover everything. The instructions included how to help him dress, when he should go to bed, what he would eat, and any other routines we had developed.

In preparing Gene for my first practice trip of two nights away, I showed him a calendar a week before the trip, marked off the days until I left, and told him I was going to TanTarA. On Memorial Day we had gone to our farm for a day's picnic with some of our family and my brother, George, and his family. The farm is very primitive with no running water, only an outhouse. It does have electricity but after our kids were grown, we hadn't been there very often.

When our kids were growing up we spent a lot of time there with my brother's family and Gene loved it. He enjoyed time on the tractor cutting the grass, fishing, and fixing things with George. In fact, he, George, a good friend, and Tom (the only kid old enough to help) built the house that we used. Before the house was built around 1968, we camped in tents.

In our early days at the farm, Gene was the resident storyteller. Before bed we would all gather around him. The kids loved his tales, although we found it funny that they always put Tom to sleep. That wasn't the case with the others. They absorbed each word. Gene was a real master at it with a vivid imagination. He used each child's name and even the names of some of the adults for the characters. Some tales were a bit gruesome, but the kids loved hearing their names. Susanna, my brother's oldest, would repeat each tale the next morning; she loved them that much. One time we decided to tape the story, but it turned out to be his worst. I guess he got stage fright.

Another of Gene's talents, along this line, was his

knack of talking like Donald Duck. The grandchildren would beg him to talk like Donald Duck and Gene would carry on a whole conversation acting like he was scolding, laughing or just talking. It was so funny and the grandchildren have fond memories of those times.

On that Memorial Day Gene, looked around the house, went upstairs, and found it pretty dirty – not someplace you would want to stay the night. So when I went on "my practice trip" to TanTarA, he thought it was to the farm and could not understand why I would take my bridge group to that dirty place.

Even after I left, he kept remarking to his caregivers in his own way that he could not understand why I wanted to stay at such a dirty place with my friends. While I was gone, he was pretty good, except that he constantly wanted to know where I was. One day he got very angry that I was not there and told Floss to get me or he would walk to where I was. I guess he did not like sleeping by himself, and was up a lot more at night than usual. He still had it in his mind that I was at the farm and that bothered him. Somehow, God gave all of us who were with Gene, an uncanny ability to ferret out what he was trying to get across to us.

Later that summer, I planned another trip, this time with Gene and our friends the Haumessers, to TanTarA. Gene did not want to go; he was still mixing up the resort with the farm. I showed him pictures of the farm and said, "NO," then showed him pictures of TanTarA and said, "YES." He wasn't buying it. I almost decided not to go, but since Pat and Arnold were kind enough to put up with us for the weekend, and I knew that once he got there he would enjoy himself, I persisted. They always paid a lot of attention to him and tried very hard to carry on a conversation with him. I figured he wouldn't notice that the eaves were not painted and that all those trees had never been topped.

However, it was a very trying three-hour drive, he fussed most of the way. A stop at McDonald's appeased him somewhat, for we both liked McDonald's. When he finally got his first glance at the lake and recognized the familiar highway into town and on to TanTarA, he was very happy and I breathed a sigh of relief. We actually had a wonderful time.

One evening as we were coming back from dinner in the dark on a lonely stretch of Highway 5, I saw out of the corner of my eye, two deer running full speed toward our moving car. There was nothing I could do except swerve a little. The first one hit the front right fender and headlight and bounced off. What happened to the second one, I have no idea. I could see headlights pretty far behind me, but since there was no shoulder and it was very dark, I didn't stop until we got into town. Fortunately no one was hurt, just jarred, and the car drove fine. However, I was amazed at the damage to the grill. I think over $2,000 worth.

I'm not sure how much of this episode even registered with Gene.

I planned a family vacation in Williamsburg, having reserved four units through our timeshare. However, the kids decided that Gene was not up to traveling. We had taken the whole family to the Dominican Republic for New Year's (2003-2004) and that didn't work out very well. Gene's hip hurt him a lot and there was too much walking for him. Tom and David were very helpful with their dad, and tried to give me a break, but it was not enjoyable. It turned out to be our last family trip with Gene.

They said they would all come into St. Louis for a long weekend, the weekend before I had planned the Williamsburg trip. This actually worked out very well and as usual we had a great time. Gene was able to enjoy the family here (as much as he was able to enjoy them), but we also had Floss come a few times to give us all a break and give Gene some peace and quiet.

Some of my friends were using the time shares in Williamsburg and there was still one left for me, so I decided I would fly (they drove) and spend a few days there with them. I left a day or so after the family left. My friends picked me up at the airport and we had such a good time. Williamsburg is a great place to visit! It was a good rest for me, but Gene did not do as well as he had done on my previous trip. The long nights were the worst for the caregivers.

In February 2005, I took a quick trip to St. Simons Island, Georgia, to visit a sorority sister. It was another practice trip, each trip a little longer to prepare Gene for my big trip in April with Dave, Marsha. and Kimmy to visit Brian who was in Germany on a Rotary scholarship. What an amazing experience for an 18-year-old! Brian stayed with two families in a small town near Hamburg. The year before Marsha had asked me to join them and I was so honored to be included that I was determined to make it work. It was a wonderful trip: Hamburg, Berlin, and Prague.

Now as I look back, I think these practice trips were backfiring, because each one I took was a little longer and Gene seemed to become more fearful and less cooperative. And of course, his disease was progressing as well. He was having trouble sleeping, would go downstairs or take a shower at 2:00 or 3:00 A.M. or try to wake me up. He'd stand at my side of the bed and look at me or tap me. I'd play possum.

It was always such a relief for me to get away and I am forever thankful to Bill, Floss's brother-in-law who stayed with Gene on the nights that I was gone. Again, Gene's caregivers were wonderful, caring people. It really does take a very special kind of person to be able to cope with a person suffering with dementia.

18
Nursing Homes

In late October of 2005, Carol and I took a day to visit nursing homes with dementia units. Being with my daughter made this job much more palatable. Gene was up and about, still able to dress and feed himself. He had given up gardening and doing most everything else, but he was still using the computer in his own fashion so that kept him busy. But I wanted to prepare for what lay ahead and our kids felt it was time.

His back had become a real problem. He had sciatica and a lot of pain in his right hip, about where his wallet would be. A chiropractor gave him some relief, but soon I was rubbing his back in that area with Bio-freeze several times every day. His caregivers learned to do that too. It gave him relief and calmed him down. We tried a cortisone shot in his spine. That was a nightmare since he could not understand nor follow directions. It took an amazing effort to get him into position. Then it did not give him any relief. We decided not to continue, although there were supposed to be a series of three shots. I wondered how we could alleviate his pain.

All the homes we visited were clean, upbeat places

until we saw the residents in stages farther along than Gene was. That was very depressing. However, we did find an ideal place with several group homes admitting only dementia patients, with room for eight or nine residents in each. It had a homelike atmosphere with a nurse on staff at all times. The staff and residents ate together at a large table at each meal. (I was even planning to cook some of his favorite meals for the group.)

It seemed so perfect. Gene and I went to several sing-a-longs at one of the homes. I was hoping to get him used to a place like that. He enjoyed the sing-a-long for a short time and then was ready to leave. I kept wondering, how am I ever going to take him to one of these places and just leave him? It was an agonizing thought, but I knew that the time was coming when just having caregivers at home was not going to be enough. We were starting to have some "all nighters" when Gene kept getting up many times during the night, and that made for a short temper on my part.

I also took him to Parc Provence in May 2005, which specializes in Alzheimer's patients. It is a beautiful facility and one of the most upscale in our community. They held support group meetings led by someone from the Alzheimer's Association. They met in the evening and the staff assured me that they could take care of Gene while I attended the discussion. I gave them a little background and they seemed to keep Gene happy during my meeting.

However, when we got in the car, he said he knew

what kind of place that was because his dad had been in one. He said he didn't think he was ready for a place like that. His comments really surprised me, especially since he spoke in such a surprisingly clear manner. His father had been at Delmar Gardens in the Independent Living section. There was nothing wrong with his brain. I thought it interesting that Gene made that connection.

A month or so later we tried it again. Gene kind of bucked when we got to the inner door. I had called earlier and said I was bringing Gene, but they did not seem prepared for him. The person who met us pulled someone out of the kitchen to shepherd Gene around when I went into the meeting.

About twenty minutes later I could see Gene through the window in the meeting room. He and a young staff member were walking around. I knew that wasn't good because with his sore hip, he would soon be hurting and crabby. There were two facilitators in our group and I asked one if she could go and check on Gene. After a while she returned and I wasn't surprised when she said they just could not do anything with him, so I got up and left with him. When we got home, he stood in front of my chair and got words out enough for me to understand, saying, "I'm not ready for a place like that!" Wow!

This facility was supposed to be for people with dementia but they did not know what to do with Gene. If I had entertained the idea of his going there on a permanent basis, I dropped it like a hot potato. This incident showed that Gene's dementia was different from the other residents. The fact that he could not talk made it harder for everyone. On the bright side, he didn't bore us with asking the same question over and over or repeating the same story over and over.

This episode made me all the more comfortable with my decision to use the Dolan Residential Care Center, which was building a new facility that would have room for nine residents. As it was being built we toured it, picked out Gene's room and thought about what furniture he would need. I even bought a cheap computer desk that Floss put together. Again she came to my rescue. I was very insistent that there be an Internet hookup for his computer. We were told that the facility would be ready for occupancy by the summer of 2007, about six months away. I figured we would both be ready by then for this transition.

With that big decision out of the way, I was asked to join a large group of women, mostly from our old neighborhood, to go on a riverboat trip up the Danube River from Budapest to Prague. This trip would be in October, 2007 so I figured that would be a perfect time for me to get away. By that time Gene should be well acclimated to his new home. However, as summer approached, having built two houses ourselves, I knew that the new Dolan home would not be ready as promised in the early summer.

Hopefully it would be ready before I left in October, but by then I realized that they didn't know when it would be ready. They were having trouble with the inspections.

As each deadline approached, deep down in my heart I was glad not to have to move Gene. Emotions can be very mixed in situations such as this. Realizing that Gene would still be at home for my trip, I set up the caregivers to cover while I was gone. It turned out to be a tough assignment for them, as Gene was pretty unmanageable at night and not great during the day. I did have a memorable time and a great break, but I knew that trip would be the last I could take until Gene was placed somewhere. He was getting increasingly harder to manage, and I wondered how much longer I could cope. However, another part of me wondered how I could transition him to a new home.

19

Nightmare

And we know that in all things God works for the good of those who love him, who have been called according to his purpose.

Romans 8:28

I have waited to write this part of the story. It is hard because it is my Nightmare. It was the overall Defining Moment and the fourth one. Years later it is still painful to recall. By Thanksgiving of 2006, Gene was less tolerant and harder to handle. We had forty-two people for dinner that day, and I'm afraid it was too confusing for him. All our family was here as well as my brother's, as had been our family tradition for many, many years.

For the most part it was easier to have people come to our home, where Gene was more comfortable and could hide in his study or go upstairs where I could rub his hip with a cream that soothed his pain. I had had several four-somes for bridge at our home during that year; thus I was home and he had a good lunch and he seemed to enjoy coming in and watching us or listening to us. He always ate the muffins or cookies I had laid out. I also had another couple, our good and faithful friends the Haumessers, over for dinner many times, giving him someone else to try to talk with.

During these later times, often he refused to eat. He'd look at his plate and turn up his nose at it. He did that when it was just us and then he began doing it when friends came over. They understood and I just tried to cope with him the best I could.

Twice, once when one of my bridge groups was at the house, Gene came in and sat in his chair by us. We all spoke to him. Then suddenly he jumped up, shocking my friends, and said, "I'm going to die." Wow, quite an explosion! I calmed him down the best I could. I probably asked him if he wanted me to rub his back or asked him if he wanted something to eat. It also happened again when the Haumessers were over for dinner. It was a bit disconcerting for all of us.

By Thanksgiving, 2006, we were still waiting for the Dolan home to be finished, five months late, and I was wondering how much longer I could cope. We were having more disruptions at night now. I would wake up in the middle of the night and find Gene in the bathroom taking off his clothes, getting ready to take his shower or trying to go downstairs. I did not feel I could trust him downstairs and was also afraid he would fall in the dark but I was certainly not ready to get up yet. Interrupted sleep was taking its toll on me.

It seemed that from Thanksgiving until January 21, 2007, something awful happened most days. On the 23rd of December 2006, Alice, one of his caregivers, was here. I realized that Gene had been in the bathroom a long time. He didn't respond to my knocking and calling. Somehow he always locked the door—I am sure he didn't know he did it—so I got that little key and went in. He was standing in front of the toilet and the water was running over the sides! He seemed to know something was wrong, so he kept flushing the toilet. I'm writing this part of his story as if I were calm, but believe me, I was not. In fact, I was panicky. I tried to get down to turn the water off, but I could not budge him out of the way.

Alice came to my assistance, we finally got Gene out of the way, and Alice was able to turn off the water. Water had gone through the floor into the finished part of the basement. I ran and got towels and rugs to sop up the water on the bathroom floor. I called Dave, my son-in-law and he came over with equipment to sop it up in the basement. We called the insurance company, who sent a professional. They pulled up the rugs and set up fans. We were having about twenty people over for Christmas Eve the next day and that bathroom was unavailable except to Gene. He didn't understand that he couldn't use it so we had to let him.

We got through that crisis, but I wondered when the next one would come. Several times, I had been so frustrated with his bathroom accidents that I would call Carol and ask her to come over and comfort me. She did, thankfully. Gene's caregivers were most helpful, but I was at the point where I didn't like to leave him too long even with them. When I was away from home, I would rush back, dreading what might have happened.

On Sunday, January 21, I had just been thinking that we had had a good day. We had had a nice dinner without disruption and without an excessive amount of hip pain. A very peaceful day. There hadn't been a lot of them, so I appreciated this one.

That evening we went upstairs to get ready for bed. Gene always watched me when he thought it was bedtime and when I made motions that I was getting up he would get up. An engineer by training and temperament, he was still very tidy. He had a place for everything and would put his shoes and all his clothes in their place. On that fateful evening, he took off a shoe and started to place it where it belonged but he could not find the other shoe. He got more and more agitated, despite the fact that I had given him his sleeping pill and an anti-anxiety pill which usually calmed him down in a very short time.

The "lost" shoe was still on his foot and I kept pointing to it and telling him it was on his foot. After ten minutes or so, he started brandishing the other shoe. I tried to stay out of his way. It was getting pretty scary. I decided I would go downstairs, hoping he would calm down but he started yelling at the top of his lungs. I went back upstairs. By now I was at my wit's end. I did not know how to handle him. It was so sad to see him this way, sort of limping around with one shoe on and waving the other one like a weapon. It was also funny in a weird sort of way. What to do?? What to do?

I thought about calling my son-in-law or my brother, but what could they do? I finally made the fateful decision to call 911. It was 11:00 P.M. and this had been going on for a half hour. It seemed like an eternity. I realized that Gene was getting more and more energized. His meds were not working. He didn't seem tired at all and I was getting more and more scared.

I asked the EMT team to come but not to have their lights or sirens on because I didn't want to wake up the neighborhood. They came quickly, two police cars and an ambulance. Gene hit them and pushed them and — I can hardly write this — they took him away. I had expected them to give him a shot to calm him down, but they had to take him to the psych ward at St. John's Hospital. It didn't occur to me when I called that he would be taken to such a place. I followed in my car and sat in the waiting room for some time. Time was now just floating. I called Carol right after I called 911, but told them not to come because I didn't know what they could do. This was a true nightmare. I guess I hoped I would wake up and find it really *was* a nightmare.

The nurse came in to the waiting room after a long time and said I could see Gene. He was sitting in a chair, trussed up. He looked at me and said very clearly, "He-lp me." He looked so sad and uncomfortable. I was devastated. It had come to this.

I tried to loosen the ties. We waited for a long time. I asked them to put him in a bed, he looked so tired sitting so tight in that chair, but the bed did not help much. They were amazed that the medicine had not knocked him out. Finally the nurse came in and said they had to transfer him somewhere else – our insurance didn't cover the psych ward at St. John's. Again, what to do?

There were several choices. The hospitals close by did not have psych wards. Several others didn't have openings. They finally found a place for him in Wentzville at St. Joseph's, SSM. It's about a thirty-five minute drive from our house, and by now it was 5:00 A.M. I had been in contact with Carol and we decided I would go home and try to get a few hours sleep and we would go out at 9:00 the next morning.

I was having three of my good friends (Nooter wives) over for bridge at 10 A.M. that day. I called one and quickly explained, asking her to call the others and asking them to come at 11:00 instead of 10:00. I knew we couldn't stay long seeing Gene and I didn't want to come home to an empty house or to be by myself or even to keep hashing it all over with Carol. I knew my friends would give me support, and bridge would take my mind off of this terrible situation. I didn't want to have a pity-party. I believe even at these awful moments, that God has a plan for those that believe in His Son. I also knew that He would not give me more than I could handle.

Visiting Gene that morning or rather seeing him (the doctors did not want family visiting so soon) was truly heart wrenching. We could only catch a glimpse of him through a one-way window. He was shuffling around in a daze. I wanted so badly to go and hug him! We talked briefly to the doctor and social worker and then left.

Gene stayed in that place for a week. He lost weight because he wouldn't eat, looked awful, and could not or would not communicate. It was agonizing visiting him and I'm not sure he knew me. After a week in Wentzville, he was released. I knew I could not handle him anymore. I had been talking to John of Dolan Residential Care (his place still was not ready). John found a place for him at one of their other facilities and said he would drive out with me to pick him up. John sat in the back seat with Gene while I drove and we both tried to talk to him. He always sat in the front seat, but I was fearful about what he might do.

Since Gene loved McDonald's hamburgers, fries and a coke, we stopped along the way to get him one. I was hoping that would make him happy. He looked so forlorn. John tried to help him eat but Gene would only take a few bites.We had not gone into McDonald's because we did not know how Gene would react. Because we never ate in the car, maybe Gene did not understand eating in the car or sitting in the backseat.

We got him settled in Mason Manor, which is located on the road we used to use to get to our home in Bellerive Estates, where we had lived for eighteen years. So at least the surroundings were familiar, although it didn't make any difference to Gene. He started eating again, but he couldn't find the bathroom and started spitting a lot. He stayed there for four weeks until the Dolan Home we had been waiting for was finally finished, now about nine months late.

My brother helped me move some of Gene's things in and arrange his room, hoping he would be happy to see familiar things. We got his computer set up and tried to be optimistic. It was a lovely place, but it was not for Gene. He became very unmanageable, up at night, and then he pulled an aide's hair. They called me and said they were sending him to the psych ward at St. Mary's Hospital. They had to sedate him so much there that he never walked again. He didn't eat but was still very strong. He stayed at St. Mary's for fifteen days until the doctors felt they had his meds regulated. He was like a zombie. The social workers at St. Mary's were very kind and helpful. John from Dolan said they would try to take him back, but I said no. I knew he was far beyond their wonderful place. They felt very bad because we had waited so long for the place to be finished, but it was too late. I am not sure Gene would have fit into a place like that anyway and probably a lot of this would have happened even if we had gotten him in months earlier as originally planned. If we had gotten him in earlier and this scenario had happened, I would have certainly blamed myself for sending him out of our home. God does have a plan.

We had another crisis. St. Mary's suggested a couple of places that might work for Gene. One was Delmar Gardens, which was very close to our home. Gene's Dad had been in the Independent Living facility across Highway 40. Carol and I went to visit and thought it would be fine. The day before he was to be taken there, I went over to sign him up and pay. I talked to a different administrator than Carol and I had seen the day before. She kept reading the transcript of Gene's history and saying something about not taking someone who was combative and that they had no tolerance for that behavior. Well, I thought, my gosh, what can we do? I couldn't be sure that Gene wouldn't be combative and I sure didn't want him back in a psych ward. I left there crying.

I couldn't get in touch with Carol, so I decided that I would drive to St. Mary's, even though it wasn't visiting hours. This was an emergency and I had to talk to them. The social worker there was very soothing. She suggested Garden View and called them. They said some of their personnel were there in the hospital and would come up and evaluate Gene, which was their normal way of assessing someone. (Delmar Gardens didn't do that. They just read a two-week-old evaluation history and didn't check on his recent progress.)

The next day, an ambulance took Gene to Garden View in Chesterfield. I was there waiting for him. He was sitting in a wheelchair and may have been pleased to see me. He was not tied in and I wish now that I had mentioned that maybe he should be. However, I learned later that the state or federal government has mandated that patients cannot be tied in unless they fall out. Now does that make sense? It's like locking the barn after the horse is stolen.

The next day, I visited him and you wouldn't believe the goose egg he had on his head. He had tried to reach down and pick something off the floor and tumbled onto his head! It seems to me that some of our government regulations cause what I would call negligence. Garden View and most other nursing homes advertise that they are a "no restraint facility." They can't do anything in the way of restraining patients until something happens. Well, from then on Gene was restrained, as only made sense. It took a long time for Gene's head to heal and it turned many colors in the process. It did not seem to bother him but it sure bothered me.

Many of the beds in Garden View are lowered to about 8" from the floor and a mattress is laid by the bed so if they fall, they fall onto the mattress. Such a system was necessary because they were not allowed to tie them in bed or even put rails up. It was explained to me that a person could scoot around the rails or go over them and that tying them down could cause bigger problems. That made sense to me. They cut down on some of Gene's psych meds and he was a little less zombie-like.

Things mostly went very smoothly at Garden View. When Gene was first admitted, the staff did not think he would last more than a few months. He was not eating and we all took turns feeding him. I visited him once a day, usually at mealtime, either lunch or dinner, so that I could feed him. I had to stay out of his spitting range. Maybe he was trying to tell us not to feed him, but of course, we couldn't stop.

Those ten months or so at Garden View gave me a chance to renew my love for him. In some ways it was a peaceful time, I did not have to worry so much. I took him for long walks in the courtyard in his wheelchair and tried to have conversations with him. I took him to sing-a-longs in their large gathering room and to their church service. I think of it as a healing time for me and hopefully he felt some of my love. I even sang to him, usually the songs we had sung at church that Sunday. I am no singer, but they came from my heart.

20

End Days

After Gene was in the nursing home for about six weeks, the nurse called to suggest that it was time for us to contact hospice. I called the kids, and then I called my friend Pat. She must have heard the catch in my voice and immediately said, "Come for dinner, nothing fancy." I dropped everything and went. It was a sweet evening.

The Fifth and last Defining Moment—when Gene entered hospice care—came on May 8, 2007. We think of the criterion for hospice care as the "end of life" coming during the next six months. The reason we called in hospice for Gene was that he wasn't eating or drinking much, and thus was losing a lot of weight. He was also spitting after he had a few bites of food. You had to be careful not to be in his line of fire! He could really project and we wondered if he sometimes aimed. At that point they did not think he would last more than a couple of months. We had heard that comment before.

Hospice started immediately on a pain management program. Apparently it helped his sciatica. Amazingly he started eating again. He was still losing weight, but he was more alert and seemed to understand more. Sometime later he started trying to carry on a conversation, which, of course, we couldn't understand, but he was trying to tell us things. I took him outside everyday when it was nice or wheeled him around the long hall when it wasn't.

One beautiful day when we were sitting outside in the courtyard with another wife and her husband, Gene started talking a blue streak. We were so excited as he carried on a long conversation. Of course, we couldn't understand anything he was saying but he was saying something. I answered with, "Really, yes, oh wow," and other meaningless phrases. Gene turned toward me and even leaned down a little like he was really listening to me and wanted to hear my response. I felt it was a real breakthrough and was comforted.

I told his aide, Nate about this and Nate remarked that Gene talked to him at bedtime like that. It was a happy day for me and I think for Gene too. I hoped it would happen again but it didn't. Thinking back, I do wonder what he was conversing about. He wasn't angry or excited, just seemingly giving us information.

Before Christmas and again for Gene's birthday on January 26th, I set up lunch for the entire Garden View staff. I wanted all of them to know how much I appreciated all that they did. Working in a place like Garden View takes a very special person, and I am so thankful for their dedication.

His caregivers at Garden View were wonderful: Adrian, Cassandra, Nate, Roberta, Jinny, Ray, and Lisa, his main nurse, as well as his other nurses and caregivers. Many times they greeted me with a report of how well he ate, or a word or two that he said. How he called my name, or cussed them out when they were giving him a shower (I can't blame him) or pulled and punched them when they were dressing or changing him. Sometimes it took two of them (I helped at times, making three of us) to do any of the above. When we were finished, we knew we had a work-out.

Gene was in hospice for more than nine months. In mid-January the hospice staff felt that his passing could come very soon. For four days, he was curled up in a ball, his blood pressure was down, he needed to be on oxygen, his skin was mottled, and there were other signs that signal to these professionals that the end was near.

However, after four days of this—I cancelled all my activities and sat with him for five and six hours a day—he rallied and started drinking and eating some. I had given him ice chips during this time, which he started chewing. This surprised us all. Maybe he had a bug that he was able to fight off with rest or maybe our Lord wasn't ready for him in heaven. I had told him that Jesus was preparing a room for him, but He hadn't finished it yet.

They took the oxygen off and got him up. He had a

very fancy and comfortable—I hoped it was comfortable for him—wheelchair. He stopped spitting so much; in fact, he hardly spit at all.

By the first of February of 2008, he was down to ninety-nine pounds. He weighed about one hundred eighty pounds when he left our home a year earlier. His highest weight in the army was two hundred fifteen pounds, but I think his normal weight was around one hundred ninety pounds.

Now, as we watched him, every three days or so his vitals would go down and they thought he would not last more than a day. Then he rallied and we continued on. It was quite a roller coaster situation for him, for me, for our family, for our friends and for all those who were praying for him. I prayed for his comfort and peace. He still got a little agitated but he was off most of his medicine except for pain medication and something for agitation, as well as his allergy medicine.

I did not know if Gene was trying to stay alive or if he knew what was going on, but I thought he was show-ing his strong will and his ability to control. I tried to keep family and friends apprised of his situation but I ran out of things to say. Sometimes I'd think he would always be with us and of course, he will be, in another form. I even had several dreams: one was that he got up and started walking and his mind was back to normal. What a wonderful happening! Sometimes, I woke up thinking he is at my side in bed!

I really could not imagine life without Gene — although I had been living by myself for over a year and actually enjoying it. However, I thought my car will just turn to the left to go to Garden View after he was gone. I visited him every day and many times had a "good" visit with him, as well as with the staff and other caregivers. My church Circle was very supportive and prayed for both of us during this time.

I wanted to plan his Memorial Service and talked to our pastor, Phil Rowland, who visited to pray for Gene and with me. His wife, Cecelia, worked with me on other parts of the arrangements and they were a great comfort. Judy Koehler, our Congregational Care Coordinator visited quite often, also. One of our young adult groups called and asked what they could do at my home to help me. I was astounded. I suggested they paint my garage doors. Some years ago Gene had decided to do some touch up, however he used a different shade of white and the doors looked awful. I never wanted to make a big deal out of something that he had tried to do that didn't turn out well, so I just ignored it. It seemed so appropriate for them to paint the doors for Gene. Every time I drive in I see those beautiful doors and remember their kindness.

I told Marsha in New York that when the time came the service would be on a weekend so that the five grandchildren in college could get here without missing too many of their classes. I mentioned that since Brian was in Rome (there with others and their professor from Dartmouth, taking classes in Italian for three months), I was sorry that he would not be able to come. Marsha said, "He's coming!" I didn't think I had heard her right and she repeated, "He's coming." I got very teary eyed and choked up. Marsha made it clear that whenever the service was to be, Brian would be there. She said that he really wanted to come. He was very close to his grandpa and had visited him last summer as well as some other times. It was hard for some of the kids to see grandpa like he was toward the end and I understood that and honored their feelings. The older grandchildren—Sam, Brian and Kimmy—had more of a relationship with their grandpa and knew him when he was well.

In mid-February, Gene began losing his ability to chew food and swallow it. He would chew and chew and then pocket the food in his mouth for maybe several hours, although other times he did chew and swallow. He was able to use a straw and drink juice and his "Cal Two." He dumbfounded the hospice staff (Regina, Ann, Dottie and Zanite) as well as the staff at Garden View. Two other hospice people visited him regularly: Chuck, a volunteer and Kathleen, the chaplain. I will be forever grateful to all those listed in this account, as well as those not mentioned. All his caregivers were unbelievably caring and supportive.

I am so thankful that these people were willing to share their gift with Gene and me. It *is* a gift to care for others, and I thank God that there are people who are willing to do this work. It is a very wearing occupation and takes a special person.

On February 27, 2008, the night nurse called me at 5:00 A.M. She thought his time had come. I had heard this for the last five weeks; nonetheless, I quickly dressed and got to Garden View before she went off her shift. I stayed eleven hours that day and watched his chest go up and down. That night after I got home and went to bed, I had the most awful pain in my left side. I figured it was diverticulitis (was I under stress?). I got out the heating pad, took some Advil, and decided I could tough it out until morning. The pain did let up, but I called my doctor and he felt I should go to the emergency room. They thought I had passed a kidney stone. Now the pain was gone and I got out of the ER in time to go to a bridge group. I felt I just couldn't go watch Gene breathe again all day and my kids didn't think I should do that either. I visited him later in the day and he was the same. My foursome bridge groups were a real antidote to my stress.

On Friday, February 29, 2008, (Leap Year Day) I got to Gene's room around noon. While the hospice aide gave him a sponge bath in bed, I watched his chest go up and down. He was stiff as a board, eyes unseeing and mouth open. She had just finished putting his undershirt on when

I noticed there was no movement. I checked his chest and the aide checked it. I got the nurse and then the head nurse, who pronounced him dead at 1:00 P.M. We were all crying, but I said, "We should be happy. I am happy, he is finally at peace."

I called Carol and she came right over. Gene had donated his brain to the Memory and Aging Project at Washington University, so they had to put ice all around his head. I knew they would do that and thought it would bother me, but I was so glad that he was at peace that I just couldn't be sad. Carol and I waited until the transporter came to take him to Washington University. I must say that he now looked in death exactly as he had looked for the last two days or more.

I had thought that no matter how long I sat with him, I would not be there when the end came, so I am so grateful to God that I was there. I even thought he tried to wiggle his tongue when I first came in and he heard my voice.

Since I had had a lot of time to plan his funeral, I made it into a celebration of Gene's life – death for Gene was a blessing and HIS LIFE WAS WELL WORTH A BIG CELEBRATION. We had the visitation at our home on a snow-covered Friday afternoon a week after his death. Visitation at home is a Jewish custom called Shiva. My son-in-law is Jewish and I have been to several Shivas and I like the custom. All the grandchildren came and maybe two hundred friends dropped by despite the bad weather and terrible roads. I was so touched. We played a video about his life, displayed dozens of photographs, and there was lots of food, thanks to friends and family. My son-in-law's mother and sisters practically catered it. My two daughters-in-law and granddaughters were enormously helpful.

On Saturday morning, we went out to the old cemetery at Dardenne Presbyterian Church in St. Charles County, where my grandparents and other relatives are buried. Our plots were marked with Gene's and my initials, so he knew long ago where his resting place would be. It was a military service with Phil Rowland saying a few comforting words and, after taps was sounded, there was a three-gun salute. Gene's casket was draped with the American flag and the officer in charge folded it up and gave it to me. As we filed out, we each put a rose on the casket. Gene loved roses. It was a very, very cold and sad day! We then went to the memorial service at Central Presbyterian Church where I have been a member since I was five years old.

All three of our children, Tom, Dave, and Carol wanted to speak at the service, and I also asked his long time Nooter friend, George Bouchaert. Each of them spoke of their memories of their dad and friend. There were many friends and family there and the whole day was most appropriate to Gene's memory.

Epilogue

Life has continued without Gene. Since I had been in the house alone for a year before he died, the adjustment to that situation was not a problem. I enjoy my home and still continue to entertain. I keep very busy. Friends have been so supportive and at my age, there are many widows who also want to stay actively involved in life. We need each other. One of the most recent, sadly, is Pat Haumesser, whose husband, Arnold, died on January 6, 2010.

I have several thoughts about Gene. First, I don't think I could do anything differently, but I know that we, mainly I, kept him alive by feeding him. I guess he was telling us that he didn't want to eat or live by spitting out so much of his food. I guess I should not have been so persistent, as was the staff at Garden View, but I certainly encouraged them to feed him. I just could not stand to see him starve. I also wonder if the Aricept and Namenda just prolonged a terrible life for him, but there again we had to do whatever was available and it seemed to be the best course of treatment at the time.

The report of the autopsy of his brain from Washington University was mailed to me a year after his death. Many pages long, it mostly says that he had plain old Alzheimer's. All the other possibilities were ruled out, but with the disease striking the part of his brain that controlled his speech first, his symptoms were different. I guess I was hoping the report would say that it was some exotic disease. Gene was special and for some reason, I never wanted to believe that he was suffering from Alzheimer's, although Dr. Morris said it was atypical.

Because such a large portion of his brain on the left side was atrophied, one theory is that he was hit in the head by a baseball when he was eleven or twelve (a long-time friend believes that this did happen), and he was able to compensate all those years. When some form of dementia set in, he no longer could compensate. The creeping nature of this disease is, I am afraid, inevitable.

I can't say that I miss Gene the way he was for his last ten years or so, but I grieve for his missing so much now. I'm sad that he never got to enjoy his retirement after working so hard all those years. He would enjoy having the time to play golf and tennis; my brother is still playing with the group that Gene played in. He would also love going to our farm, my brother George's now

He and George were best friends. He could drive the tractor and fish to his heart's content. He could tell his wonderful tales to his grandchildren, and talk like Donald Duck.

I miss that we can't share our experiences with each other each day. Of course, that had not been possible for a long time.

George Johnson - Betty's Brother

I realize now that I loved him so much, that he was a very good and honest man. I relive some of our early loving years. Early in our marriage we made a pact to never say the "d" word (divorce), even if we were kidding. We both felt that divorce could never be an option. I wish young people today looked at marriage that way: "Until death do us part." However, death has parted us and I still feel married and still wear my rings. He was a good husband, a good father, a good grandfather, and a good friend to many. What more can one say! Rest in peace, Gene, and I know that you are in Heaven.

God gave me the ability to accept our situation and the wisdom to see that no one is immune from bad situations. It's not, "Why is this happening to us?" but "Why not us?" I feel God has truly blessed us in many ways.

I frequently remember the Bible verse which tells us that God does not give us more then we can bear if we believe in Him and are doing his will. His grace is sufficient.

No test or temptation that comes your way is beyond the course of what others have had to face. All you need to remember is that God will never let you down; he'll never let you be pushed past your limit; he'll always be there to help you come through it.

1 Corinthians 10:13   (The Message)

Case History

AUTOMATED ASSESSMENT OF ATROPHY PROGRESSION IN A CASE OF PROGRESSIVE APHASIA

RL Buckner, AZ Snyder, L William, BT Gold, SD Sergent-Marshall, DA Balota, and JC Morris
Washington University in St. Louis, Washington University School of Medicine, Howard Hughes Medical Institute

GENE'S CASE HISTORY

At age 64 y, this RH retired Executive and college graduate was first evaluated in the Memory and Aging Project (MAP) at Washingon University. He had no serious medical problems and his only prescription medicine was a PRN drug for "allergies". There was no history of head trauma or alcohol or drug misuse. Neither the patients's parents nor siblings (both older) had language, cognitive or neuropsychiatric problems.

The history indicated that at about age 58 y, the patient gradually developed language difficulties. Symptoms were described as lessened ability to understand conversations and unaccustomed word-finding problems gradually progressed and began to be an embarrassment in social settings and at work. He eventually was unable to lead Board meetings or orally present at company events;

he "retired" at age 64 because of the language problems.

When the patient was about age 62 y, the wife noted that he also was becoming forgetful. Although at first this seemed minor (forgetting trivial conversations), by age 64 y he had experienced geographic disorientation and had problems recalling telephone numbers and keeping score in tennis. He was less able to play card games (bridge), made errors paying the bill at restaurants, and was a less safe driver; he received two speeding citations.

He was evaluated by a neurologist at age 63 y. The examination revealed impaired fluency, dysnomia, occasional paraphasic errors, and dysgraphia. The examination otherwise was unremarkable, as were standard laboratory values (eg, thryroid functions test, vitamin B12 level, serum chemistries). A more extensive evaluation was performed at another institution. Diminished repetition, impaired naming and spelling, and rare paraphasic errors were noted, as was dyscalculia. Among other procedures, DSG studies and a heavy metal screen (urine) were unrevealing. Neuropsychological examination reported relative preservation of memory and learning with impaired language, attention and visuoperceptual abilities.

At the MAP evaluation, he remained capable in many respects; he recently had made repairs to his kitchen floor, appropriately selecting and purchasing needed items. He correctly used appliances such as a coffee maker. He drove without accident. He was independent in all aspects of self-care. His neurologic examination was unremarkable; specifically, graphesthesia and stereognosis were intact, there was no right-left disorientation or finger agnosia, and all reflexes were symmetric with flexor plantar responses. On brief cognitive testing, he recalled a 5-item memory phrase correctly, serially subtracted 3 from 20, and stated that there were "27" quarters in $6.75 but made one error in reciting months backward and was unable to correctly draw a clock. He also had errors in recalling a recent event in which he had participated. The language examination was marked by diminished spontaneous speech, mild dysnomia, inability to repeat appropriately and dysgraphia. He was diagnosed with primary progressive aphasia (primarily nonfluent) of 6 years duration with subsequent very mild "global" dementia (Clinical Dementia Rating = 0.5) of 3 years duration.

His language and cognitive difficulties gradually progressed; at age 65, a cholinesterase inhibitor was prescribed and has been tolerated without problem. By age 69 y (5/02), his speech was stuttering, hesitant, and generally empty of content. He could follow spoken one-step but not two-step commands. He was unable to name objects, repeat, or read a simple sentence. He could no longer write. He did not know his age. He was responsible for his medication and remained independent in self-care except that he required assistance with tying his necktie. The diagnosis remained primary progressive nonfluent aphasia with mild "global" dementia (Clinical Dementia Rating = 1, based on his nonverbal functioning). The underlying cause(s) of his condition are believed to be atypical Alzheimer disease versus frontotemporal lobar degeneration.

CONCLUSIONS

The disproportionate language impairment in this mildly demented individual most likely relates to premorbid hemispheric asymmetry–namely, clinically silent left hemispheric atrophy. This case study raises the possibility that certain atypical presentations of dementia, such as those that appear as primary progressive aphasia, reflect different baseline states rather than progressive lobar atrophy.

Reprinted with permission from Elsevier from The Neurobiology of Aging supplement, July-August 2002.

This case history was delivered at a medical seminar in Stockholm, Sweden in 2002 and included many images of Gene's brain from many MRIs. Gene realized that these MRIs would not help him but were to be used for further study and he graciously took part.

Acknowledgments

E xcerpts of this book were first read to the Writer's Group at the Wednesday Club. They made suggestions and spurred me on. So I thank all those members.

Then the first draft was read by Pat Haumesser, who with her husband, Arnold, are a big part of the book. She helped me with some of the grammar as well as telling me how much she enjoyed reading it and thought it could be named the "Love Story".

A Nooter wife and bridge buddy, Dodie Frank had wonderful suggestions and gave me the name of an editor, Betty Burnett. (She has to be good with a name like Betty.)

Then Carol, my daughter, read it before Thanksgiving of '09. Wednesday night she called at 10:15 PM, quite late. She had just read up to the Gracie Chapter and was so touched by the whole story. The next day, Thanksgiving, as I'm preparing for only thirty-two people, she drops in. We go into my study and she hugs me saying, "Thank you for writing this". She had just been out to the Cemetery, first time since Gene's stone was erected, and planted some tulips. We cried!

Carol had some great suggestions – to add the Duffy's Chapter and best of all, Jordan, my granddaughter, read the first page or so and said I needed a hook and that I should start with the screeching brakes. I rewrote that beginning.

My thanks go to my proofreaders, Shirley Johnson, my sister-in-law; Joan Langenberg, Dodie Frank and my daughter-in-law, Marsha Smith. They tirelessly corrected punctuation, grammar, typos and spelling. I cannot forget to mention my "twin", Joan Kniest, (we were born on the same day and have Campbell as our middle names). She has been such a positive encourager and listener, as have many others.

I also want to thank my granddaughter, Lauren Smith, for the cover design and fitting it into her very busy schedule. Thanks goes to my son-in-law, Dave Roodman for using his photographic expertise to produce my picture for the back cover.

Betty Burnett, my editor has been invaluable in helping me through this whole process and now that we have met with the Publisher, Jeff Fister, whose mother is a member of the Wednesday Club, we are close to the end. Now I want to give credit to my Lord and Savior, Jesus Christ.

If this book helps only one person in some way, I will be forever grateful.

Betty J. Smith

About the Author

Betty Johnson Smith, a St. Louis native, graduated from Southwest High School and Washington University. She taught school for a short time, married Gene Russell Smith, raised three children and was active in the Delta Gamma Center for Children with Visual Impairments as well as her Church and her children's schools. This is her first book.